Say goodbye to boring salads.

Life-Changing Salads is more than just a cookbook—it's your ultimate guide to creating satisfying, plant-based salads that you'll crave. From crunchy chopped salads to cozy warm bowls, hearty salad wraps, quinoa powerhouses, and even no-lettuce salads (perfect for meal prep), every salad situation is covered!

With creative recipes like the spring roll salad and the Caesar pasta salad, you'll never feel stuck in a salad rut again. Discover how to create creamy, indulgent dressings using nondairy yogurt or hummus, whip up nutrient-packed superfood blends, and master satisfying textures using nuts and seeds— all without compromising on flavor.

Whether you're new to plant-based eating or simply looking to level up your salad game, *Life-Changing Salads* will inspire you to make these vibrant, nutrient-dense meals a staple in your kitchen. With over 100 recipes for irresistible salads and essential dressings, this is the only salad guide you'll ever need. Let's get chopping!

life-changing
SALADS

life-changing
SALADS

100 plant-based salads and dressings
beyond your wildest greens

danielle brown

Publisher Mike Sanders
Executive Editor Alexander Rigby
Art & Design Director William Thomas
Editorial Director Ann Barton
Senior Designer Jessica Lee
Recipe Photographer Ari Brown
Lifestyle Photographer Amanda Julca
Co-Recipe Developer Taylor Hubschman
Recipe Tester Laura Manzano
Development Editor Tiffany Taing
Copy Editor Monica Stone
Editorial Assistant Resham Anand
Proofreaders Jaye Whitney Debber, Claire Safran
Indexer Johnna VanHoose Dinse
Makeup Artist Cameron Krigel
Cover Image Stylist Brandon Hubschman
Dressing Photographer & Stylist Kelly Rodenhouse
Lifestyle Shoot Food Stylist Adriana Paschen

First American Edition, 2025
Published in the United States by DK Publishing
1745 Broadway, 20th Floor, New York, NY 10019

The authorized representative in the EEA is Dorling Kindersley
Verlag GmbH. Arnulfstr. 124, 80636 Munich, Germany

A catalog record for this book
is available from the Library of Congress.
ISBN 978-0-5939-6183-4

DK books are available at special discounts when purchased
in bulk for sales promotions, premiums, fund-raising, or
educational use. For details, contact SpecialSales@dk.com

Printed and bound in China

www.dk.com

This cookbook is dedicated to my Aidan.
You are the reason I wake up every day.
Thank you for making me a mama.

Contents

go-to salads

fruit salads

grain salads

no-lettuce salads

dressings

Introduction

Welcome to *Life-Changing Salads*. I'm Danielle, the *New York Times* best-selling cookbook author of *HealthyGirl Kitchen*, and I'm here to teach you the secrets to plant-based eating without feeling restricted or deprived. If you want to make a real change, it's time to stop following diets and time to start a healthy lifestyle.

I am going to teach you how to make the most amazing salads, from the best dressings you'll ever have, to the most efficient methods for meal-prepping salads. Not only will you learn how to make savory salads, but I'll also show you how to make perfect fruit salads.

Filled with fiber, protein, and healthy fats, my salad recipes will keep you satiated and energized, support digestion and gut health, and make you glow from the inside out.

This book will leave you feeling a lot more confident in the kitchen. I always say that I'm not a chef; I'm just a girl who likes to cook (and eat!). You're going to be nourishing your body one salad at a time.

Why a Life-Changing Salads Book?

In 2022, I started sharing my salad recipes on social media in a series called *Life-Changing Salads*. The series soon went viral, and millions of people started watching, saving, sending, liking, and following my salad series. These salads weren't fancy or complicated—they were simple and easy to follow with ingredients that were accessible, and the best part was that they tasted like they were from a restaurant, but were actually healthy and nutrient dense. I realized there was a massive need for salad tutorials that were 30 seconds or shorter and recipes that were approachable and relatable.

When buying salad dressings from a store, I noticed many were filled with seed oils, sugar, ingredients I couldn't pronounce, and dairy or eggs. I decided making my own dressings would be much more cost efficient and would also have simpler ingredients that would taste delicious and be so easy to make.

Why a Plant-Based Diet?

After struggling with my own health issues from the time I was in high school—from hormonal acne to chronic digestive issues like daily heartburn—I knew I needed to make a change. My quest for health led to me discovering a plant-based diet. I stopped eating animal products in 2014 during my freshman year of college. After a few months of eating tofu instead of meat; beans and lentils in place of eggs; and nuts, seeds, fruits, vegetables, and whole grains instead of dairy and fish, my health simply transformed. I literally had chronic heartburn for two years, and after four months of plant-based eating, the heartburn was eliminated for good. I've made it my mission to help people improve their health and well-being with a plant-centered diet, just as I did for myself.

The majority of my audience is actually not vegan—they simply want to learn how to have a meatless Monday, how to incorporate tofu into a meal in place of chicken, how to create dairy-free dressings, or how to realistically include plants as a staple on your plate. Even just one plant-based meal a day can make a huge difference in your health.

In Western culture, it seems as though you cannot find a salad anywhere without animal products. Caesar salads often come with eggs and fish in the dressing and Parmesan on top, while Cobb salads come with hard-boiled eggs and bacon. Other salads typically offer protein options like steak, fish, or grilled chicken, without tofu or another vegan option, like lentils. The lack of options leaves me unable to order great plant-based salads when I'm eating out. So I decided to take matters into my own hands and created satiating salads (75 to be exact) that taste just as good, if not better, than the ones with steak and goat cheese.

Let me preface this and say: You do not have to be vegan to enjoy the salads in this book. These recipes are for everyone!

Salad FAQ

How Long Do Salads Keep in the Fridge?

Unless you're one of the few people who enjoys soggy next-day salads, there are many tips and tricks that can help prolong the life of your salads in the fridge.

- Keep the dressing separate from the salad, and add dressing only when you are ready to eat.

- Add ingredients like avocado only when you are ready to eat the salad, since avocado can quickly get brown and mushy.

- Store premade salads in the fridge in airtight containers.

- After washing your salad greens well, make sure to dry them with a salad spinner. Wet lettuce will not store well in the fridge and will not hold dressing very well either.

- Each specific salad recipe in this cookbook will indicate whether it's leftover friendly and how long it will last in the fridge.

Can a Salad Be a Complete Meal?

Absolutely! If you are looking for your salad to be your complete meal, make sure it has protein, fat, and carbohydrates. However, you can add protein to almost any salad in this book (aside from the fruit salads) to make it a complete meal. The salads in *Life-Changing Salads* are filling, satisfying, and packed with plant protein, fiber, vitamins, and minerals.

How Do You Prepare Lettuce for a Salad?

1. Buy fresh lettuce! Make sure it's not wet, soggy, moldy, or wilted when you buy it from a store or farmers' market.

2. Remove the outer leaves from the head of the lettuce if they appear to be wilted or damaged in any way.

3. Separate the lettuce leaves from the base. Rinse the leaves in cold water until all dirt and debris are removed.

4. Dry the lettuce. I highly recommend drying the leaves in a salad spinner!

5. Cut up or tear the dried lettuce leaves with your hands. (This is up to personal preference.)

6. Super busy? Just buy prewashed, precut lettuce. That is totally fine.

What If I Don't Have a Salad Spinner?

Not to worry! While it is lovely to have a salad spinner, you can wash your lettuce, put it on a clean dish towel, then pat it dry with another clean dish towel. We do not want waterlogged lettuce—it will make for a soggy salad. No one wants that.

How Do You Store Greens Properly in the Fridge?

- One of the best-kept secrets is to keep your greens wrapped in a paper towel in the fridge after they are washed and dried. The paper towel draws out any excess moisture and keeps the lettuce fresh longer.

- You can dampen the paper towel slightly. Then wrap your greens inside the damp towel and store in a zipper-lock bag or an airtight container.

- Keep greens in the crisper drawer of your refrigerator, since it maintains an optimal environment.

- Got leafy greens? Store them on the higher-humidity setting in your refrigerator's crisper drawer.

- If your greens get slimy or moldy, throw them out. I recommend eating your greens within 4 days of storing them.

How Do I Pick the Freshest Produce and Ingredients?

- **Tomatoes:** Ripe tomatoes will vary in color depending on the variety, but using smell and touch as a guide is my trick to knowing whether a tomato is ripe. Gently press on the tomato—it shouldn't be rock hard, but it also shouldn't be super mushy. It should have a very slight give. The tomato should also smell fresh. That is the sign of a properly harvested tomato!

- **Cucumber:** To choose the best cucumber, make sure it's not slimy and doesn't have any signs of mold or mush. Gently press on the ends, and double check that it's not mushy at all. The cucumber should be nice, firm, and crisp.

- **Avocado:** A perfect avocado won't be too hard or very mushy. It will have a bit of give when pressed. If you want avocados for the week, you can buy them when they're hard, leave them on the counter to ripen, and enjoy them when they soften and produce a give when pressed.

- **Melons:** Ripe melons will offer up a sweet, aromatic melon aroma. If you hold a melon up to your nose and smell nothing, chances are it is not ripe. Melons like cantaloupe or honeydew will have a slight give when they're ripe. A cantaloupe that is green is not ripe. My trick to know if watermelon is ready is to give it a few knocks with your knuckles. If the resulting sounds are deep and hollow, it's perfect.

- **Pineapple:** Skin and smell are the most important with a pineapple. If it's ready to eat, it should smell sweet. The skin will also turn yellow when it's ready; in contrast, the skin will be green if it's not quite ripe.

- **Pasta:** When shopping, look at the bag of pasta to see if it's labeled with either "Product of Italy" or "Made in Italy." Those options will be made with higher-quality ingredients. That is my best pasta hack! I also recommend buying organic pasta. The variety of pastas available these days is great, so feel free to try out different kinds, like lentil, chickpea, whole wheat, or even edamame pasta. If buying traditional pasta, the ingredients should be 100 percent durum wheat semolina.

- **Olive oil:** The secrets to buying the best of nature's liquid gold include making sure the bottle reads "extra-virgin," checking the harvest date, ensuring the oil is fresh (less than 18 months old), seeing if the oil is in a dark bottle (which means it's good quality), and looking for cold-pressed olive oil (meaning the nutrients are better preserved). Olive oil is a staple for great salads and can be found in the majority of dressings.

- **Vinegars:** Having a few staple vinegars in your pantry will help with making daily salads. A general rule of thumb for selecting good vinegar is to choose one that comes in a glass bottle, since it will generally be better quality than those in plastic. I like to buy organic vinegars, as well. A great place to find good vinegars is at your local farmers' market.

Here are some tips for buying specific types of vinegar:

» **Balsamic vinegar:** When it comes to balsamic, the thicker, the better. If you can find a balsamic variety that's been aged for at least 12 years, you've hit the jackpot. Of course, a balsamic variety that has been aging for longer will come at a higher price point. If you are buying a cheap balsamic, it likely hasn't been aged and will be thinner as a result.

» **Wine vinegars:** Look for wine vinegars with minimal ingredients and no added sugars or artificial additives. Aged wine vinegars will be higher quality.

» **Rice vinegars:** Rice-wine vinegar offers a mild and sweet flavor and is my favorite to use in Asian-inspired salads. While there are different rice vinegars, I like to use white rice vinegar for salad dressings. I personally don't like to buy seasoned rice vinegar, because it has extra sugar and salt that I find unnecessary. Check the bottle for the origin; higher-quality rice vinegars come from places like Korea, Japan, or China.

» **Apple cider vinegar:** Choose one that is "with the mother," which indicates it is raw and unfiltered. The best part is that it's beneficial for gut health!

Should I Buy Organic or Nonorganic Produce?

Buying organic produce is a highly controversial debate. If you are in the United States and if you can afford to buy organic, I would recommend doing so when possible. But let's be honest: It can be much more expensive to buy everything organic.

A lot of people opt to buy organic produce for any item that is directly sprayed and doesn't have an outer protective skin or peel that can be removed, such as berries, greens, potatoes, lettuce, pears, or apples. For other produce with a removeable skin or peel, like bananas, avocados, or watermelon, they purchase nonorganic.

What's better is if you can find a local farmer who doesn't use any pesticides or herbicides. I have a great local farm that I love going to, and I know they have nontoxic practices when it comes to their farming.

Don't want to buy organic food at all? No worries! Just wash your produce well either way.

How to reduce pesticide exposure

- Wash all your produce before eating it!
- Use a bristle brush for firmer fruits and veggies, like cucumbers or potatoes, to brush and clean the outer layer.
- Remove the outer leaves of lettuce and cabbages.
- Buy fruit-and-vegetable wash at a local health-food store. Can't find any? Make your own! (See DIY natural fruit-and-vegetable wash, below.)
- Every year, the Environmental Working Group publishes the "Dirty Dozen" and the "Clean Fifteen" lists. Follow their guidelines for which fruits and vegetables to purchase organic or nonorganic.

DIY natural fruit-and-vegetable wash

1. Mix ¼ cup white vinegar with 4 cups water and 2 teaspoons baking soda.
2. Soak your fruits and veggies in the cleaning solution for 1 to 2 minutes. (Don't soak raspberries—they will get mushy—just rinse them.)
3. Rinse the fruits and veggies with clean water after soaking. This method will remove the majority of pesticide residues, as well as any potentially harmful bacteria on the surface of your produce.

How to Use This Book

This book is going to be your plant-based salad-making bible.

It will provide you with the blueprint for how to make everything from pasta and fruit salads to grain and chopped salads. This isn't just a cookbook you're going to use on an occasional holiday or when you have guests. This is an everyday book for the everyday person. Use this cookbook to find recipes for weekly lunch meal prep, a work potluck, a brunch spread, a weekend family gathering, a girlfriends' book club, or a side dish to have with dinner.

Most importantly, use this book in good health. Use it to make memories with friends and to learn how to make the heartiest, yummiest, most nutrient-dense salads so you can live your healthiest plant-based life.

Nutrition Info

Scan the QR code below for recipe nutrition information, including calories and macronutrients.

Recipe Labels

I am all about making cooking easy and making recipes as easy as possible for you to follow. You will find these labels listed above each recipe:

30 = ready in 30 minutes or less

h = hosting (great for entertaining)

lf = leftover friendly

nc = no cooking required

nf = nut-free

sf = soy-free

All recipes are gluten-free optional.

Essential Salad Equipment

- **Salad spinner:** This helpful device is perfect for washing and drying those dirty greens.

- **Large wood cutting board:** To avoid microplastics in your food, use a wood cutting board every time you make a salad.

- **Chef's knife:** A dull knife is a dangerous knife. A sharp good-quality knife or knife set goes a long way.

- **Salad tongs:** Tossing your salad is much easier with tongs.

- **Large salad bowl:** A big bowl is your go-to for making sizable salads.

- **Salad serving bowls:** You need something to serve your salads in!

- **Jars:** These are perfect for shaking and storing dressings.

- **Handheld salad chopper:** You can buy a salad chopper to chop your salad ingredients quickly and without a knife.

- **Measuring cups:** These come in handy when following the recipes in this book.

- **Vegetable peeler:** A peeler is essential for vegetables like potatoes and beets, but it can also be used to make vegetable ribbons out of items like cucumbers or carrots.

- **Mandoline:** This is the secret tool for getting consistently thin-sliced vegetables.

- **Grater:** You need one to grate cheese and veggies with ease.

- **Blender:** To blend many of the nut- and seed-based dressings, this item is a must. A high-speed blender, like a Vitamix, is even better, but at the end of the day, any blender will work.

- **Baking sheets and parchment paper:** A lot of these recipes start with a baking sheet lined with parchment paper. I like using parchment paper because it allows for a no-mess recipe.

HealthyGirl Kitchen
Instagram Follower FAQ

Q: What is the best way to add plant-based protein to a salad?

A: The easiest proteins to add to a salad are grilled or air-fried tofu or lentils.

Q: Is it true that darker greens are healthier than lighter greens?

A: Yes! The rumors are true. Darker greens, like kale or spinach, are far more nutrient dense than pale greens, like iceberg or romaine.

Q: How far in advance can one make a salad?

A: Pay attention to the "leftover friendly" recipes in this book, which are marked with "lf." These recipes will keep best in the fridge, so you can feel confident making them in advance. You can also preserve a salad further by keeping the dressing on the side until you're ready to eat it.

Q: **How do you organize yourself in an efficient way for buying ingredients?**

A: I recommend sitting down on a Sunday, choosing the salads you want to make for the week, then buying only the ingredients you need. Don't go to the store without a plan—you'll end up with ingredients that go to waste because you didn't have an intention for them.

Q: **Do you have tips for making quick and cheap salads in the morning?**

A: This will save you: Make your salad the night before! Prepare a leftover-friendly (lf) salad from this cookbook, like a pasta salad or a no-lettuce salad, and keep it in an airtight container in the fridge, then put it in your lunch box in the morning. Keep the dressing separate for extra freshness. In college, I used to double what I was making for dinner so I could have a portion for lunch the next day—it was the best hack.

Q: **What ingredients almost always pair well together?**

A: • Avocado and kale
  • Feta and sun-dried tomato
  • Fruit, mint, and lime
  • Romaine, black beans, and corn
  • Carrot and cucumber
  • Cabbage and bell pepper
  • Roasted sweet potato, tofu, and chickpeas
  • Quinoa, roasted veggies, and dressing

Q: **What are soy-free and nut-free protein options for salads?**

A: You can add black beans or chickpeas (garbanzo beans) to any salad. Many grocery stores sell soy-free tofu made from pumpkin seeds or fava beans. You can also add protein by incorporating hemp seeds, whether you sprinkle them on or make a hemp-seed-based dressing.

Q: **How much dressing are you supposed to use?**

A: This is completely personal. I am a dressing girl. I like a generous amount. I don't want my veggies swimming in it, but I do like full coverage, so use however much you like. Do what you have to do to enjoy your salad.

Q: **What is needed for a basic vinaigrette?**

A: I am going to make your life super easy. Truly, all you need is good-quality olive oil and a vinegar of choice, like balsamic or white wine vinegar. These two ingredients will get you far. If you want to jazz it up a little, you could add Dijon mustard and a touch of maple syrup.

Q: **How do you make prepping salads and veggies less of a chore?**

A: Light a candle before you begin, do it with a friend or your partner, get your kids involved, make a fun cooking playlist, get cute meal-prep containers, and find recipes you are actually excited to make. Any of these things will help!

Our Vegan Family

I never in a million years thought my husband would become vegan. He used to be the biggest meat eater, and meat was a part of every one of his meals. In college, he'd have a seven-egg omelet for breakfast, a bowl of ground beef and eggs for lunch, and a steak for dinner. You can imagine my surprise when, about 6 months after I made the transition to eating fully plant-based, Ari followed suit. He instantly felt better, more energized, and lighter. He loved it and never looked back. We've both been plant-based and ethically vegan since 2014. To clarify, our decision to eat plant-based isn't just for our health, it is all encompassing—for the welfare of the animals and the sustainability of our environment too.

We agreed that we'd raise a vegan family and that we'd feed our children the same food we eat. I got pregnant with our son, Aidan, in 2022, and had a beautiful vegan pregnancy. My bloodwork was great, I felt energized, and Aidan grew ahead of schedule in the womb. He was born 7 pounds 14 ounces. I started breastfeeding immediately, and my plant-based diet contributed greatly to my healthy, over-abundant milk supply. Aidan grew quickly and was always topping the charts with both his weight and height at every pediatrician appointment.

At 6 months old, Aidan began eating solids. He's open-minded about trying new foods, some of which he likes, some of which he doesn't, but he's a plant-powered kid who's thriving. It is crucial to feed all children a well-balanced diet whether they're vegan or not. We offer Aidan a variety of proteins, complex carbohydrates, healthy fats, and fruits or veggies at every meal. He loves tofu, protein pasta, raspberries, peppers, cucumber slices, roasted sweet potatoes, raisins, whole grain toast with almond cream cheese, overnight oats with peanut butter—you name it! This is what works for us, and he's a happy, healthy kid!

Our habits and lifestyle have rubbed off on our family and friends, and so many of those close to us now eat a plant-centered diet. I am constantly making my recipes and life-changing salads for my family, and now, you can make them for yours.

go-to

SALADS

the salads you'll make on *repeat*

chinese no-chicken salad

SERVES 4

Make this leftover friendly by omitting the romaine and
leaving the crunchy noodles on the side!

prep time:
20 minutes

cook time:
5 minutes

1 tbsp olive oil

1 block firm high-protein tofu,
shredded

Salt and ground black pepper,
to taste

2 cups chopped romaine or
green-leaf lettuce

2 cups finely shredded Napa
cabbage

1 cup finely shredded purple
cabbage

1 cup shredded carrots

⅔ cup thinly sliced green onions

½ cup mung bean sprouts

1 (10.5oz/297g) can mandarin
oranges, drained and rinsed

¼ cup chopped roasted and
salted almonds

2 tbsp toasted sesame seeds

2 batches **Sesame Vinaigrette**
(page 201)

½ cup crunchy noodles

1. In a large nonstick pan over medium-high
   heat, add the olive oil and shredded tofu,
   and sauté until golden brown. Season lightly
   with salt and pepper. Set aside and let cool.

2. To a large serving bowl, combine the lettuce,
   Napa cabbage, purple cabbage, carrots,
   green onions, mung bean sprouts, drained
   mandarin oranges, almonds, and sesame
   seeds.

3. Transfer the cooked tofu into the bowl.

4. Toss all ingredients with Sesame Vinaigrette.

5. Top the salad with the crunchy noodles at
   the end so they stay crisp, and enjoy!

> **Note**
> Shred the tofu with a cheese grater like you would
> a block of cheese. For the mandarin oranges,
> I recommend you get the ones canned in
> water rather than syrup. Lastly, you can
> buy preshredded carrots and other veggies
> to make your meal prep even easier.

fattoush salad

SERVES 6

This is hands down one of my favorite salads. It's crisp, fresh, herbaceous, and the perfect combination of savory and tangy. Fun fact: fattoush salad originated in Lebanon, where farmers would combine their fresh harvest and stale bread to make a hearty meal. Let's all thank these Lebanese farmers for the absolutely genius idea of turning stale pita into chips and adding them to a salad.

prep time:
15 minutes

cook time:
15 minutes

2 whole-wheat pita breads, cut into 1-in (2.5-cm) squares

Olive oil cooking spray

2 tsp za'atar seasoning blend

4 cups chopped romaine lettuce

1 cup diced tomato

1 large red bell pepper, ribs and seeds removed, diced

1 large green bell pepper, ribs and seeds removed, diced

1 large cucumber, diced

1 cup thinly sliced radishes

½ cup chopped fresh curly parsley

1 cup crumbled vegan feta cheese

1 batch **Mediterranean Mama Dressing** (page 206)

1. Preheat the oven to 400°F (200°C). Line a baking sheet with parchment paper.

2. To a medium mixing bowl, add the pita squares and spray with olive oil cooking spray, then sprinkle za'atar over the top. Mix the pita with your hands to coat evenly with the oil and seasoning. Spread the pita squares onto the parchment-lined baking sheet. Bake for 8 to 12 minutes, or until crispy. Take care not to let the pita chips burn. Set aside.

3. While the homemade pita chips bake, in a large bowl, combine the romaine, tomato, bell peppers, cucumber, radishes, parsley, and crumbled feta cheese.

4. To the assembled salad, add the crispy pita chips. Pour as much or as little dressing as you want over top. Toss and serve.

> **Note**
> Don't want soggy salad the next day?
> Add dressing only to the salad portion
> you are going to immediately eat.

buffalo "chicken" salad

SERVES 3

I think we should all come to the unanimous conclusion that buffalo chicken on a salad is a classic, delicious combination. My plant-based version is made with tofu instead of chicken, but it's crispy, spicy, delicious, and incredibly yummy when paired with a fresh salad.

prep time:
15 minutes

cook time:
25 minutes

4 cups chopped green-leaf lettuce

1 cup shredded carrots

1 large avocado, pit and skin removed, cubed

⅓ cup sliced red onion

1 cup diced cucumber

1 pint halved cherry tomatoes

1 batch **ValleyGirl Ranch Dressing** (page 234)

2 tbsp buffalo sauce

2 tbsp chives

For the buffalo chicken tofu

1 block extra-firm tofu, pressed and cubed

2 tbsp potato starch or cornstarch

1 tbsp olive oil

1 tsp garlic powder

1 tsp smoked paprika

1 tsp salt

¼ cup buffalo sauce (your favorite kind!)

1. **Make the buffalo chicken tofu.** Preheat the oven or air fryer to 425°F (220°C). If using the oven, line a baking sheet with parchment paper.

2. To a bowl, add the tofu cubes, potato starch, olive oil, garlic powder, smoked paprika, and salt. Mix until evenly coated, then place the coated cubes onto the lined baking sheet or into the air fryer.

3. Bake for 25 minutes or air-fry for 15 minutes until crispy. Remove from the oven or air fryer.

4. In a bowl, mix the crispy tofu with ¼ cup of buffalo sauce, ensuring it's coated evenly. Set aside.

5. **Prepare the salad.** To a large salad bowl, add the lettuce, carrots, avocado cubes, red onion slices, diced cucumber, and cherry tomato halves.

6. Mix 1 batch ValleyGirl Ranch Dressing with 2 tablespoons of buffalo sauce to make a creamy buffalo ranch. Toss the salad with the dressing.

7. Lastly, top the salad with the buffalo chicken tofu. Garnish with chives, and enjoy!

california roll in a bowl

SERVES 3–4

If you love ordering a California roll when you're out having sushi, this recipe is for you, baby. California rolls typically have crab in them, so I made a plant-based version of spicy crab using hearts of palm, which make a great crab substitute—your mind is going to be blown. This is basically a deconstructed sushi roll with my own little HealthyGirl twist. Ari and I love making these for date nights in.

prep time:
25 minutes

cook time:
25 minutes

1 cup short-grain sushi rice

1 (14oz/397g) can hearts of palm, drained

1 tbsp sriracha

2 tbsp vegan mayonnaise or plain vegan yogurt

2 tbsp rice vinegar

1 tsp cane sugar or maple syrup

1 large cucumber, thinly sliced

1 cup diced fresh mango

1–2 large carrots, shaved into ribbons using a vegetable peeler

1 large avocado, pit and skin removed, cubed

1 cup edamame, shelled and steamed

1 sheet roasted nori, shredded

1 batch **Carrot Ginger Dressing** (page 229)

Pinch of sesame seeds

Fresh cilantro leaves

1. In a medium pot, prepare the sushi rice according to package instructions. (It usually requires 2 cups water for every 1 cup rice.) Fluff with a fork and set aside.

2. To a medium bowl, add the hearts of palm, sriracha, and vegan mayo. Mash with a fork until well combined.

3. In a small bowl, combine the rice vinegar and sugar. Stir to combine. Add the vinegar mixture to the cooked rice and stir to combine.

4. Assemble your California roll in a bowl by adding seasoned rice to the bottom of a small serving bowl, followed by the cucumber, mango, carrot ribbons, avocado cubes, edamame, shredded nori, and hearts-of-palm "crab." Drizzle the Carrot Ginger Dressing over the top. Garnish with sesame seeds and cilantro, and enjoy!

glow bowl

SERVES 2

From the antioxidants in the beet dressing to the powerhouse of nutrients in the sprouts, and from the healthy fats in the pumpkin seeds to vitamins A and C in the squash and greens, this bowl will make you glow from the inside out. Each ingredient in this bowl is functional and will nourish every cell in your body. This kind of salad has been a staple in my diet, and my skin has never looked better.

prep time:
10 minutes

cook time:
20 minutes

1 large yellow squash, diced

1 large red bell pepper, ribs and seeds removed, diced

1 can chickpeas, drained and rinsed

1 tbsp olive oil

½ tsp salt

½ tsp ground black pepper

2 cups mixed salad greens

2 tbsp pumpkin seeds

½ cup alfalfa sprouts

1 batch **Anti-Inflammatory Beet Dressing** (page 209)

1. Preheat the oven to 400°F (200°C).

2. Line a baking sheet with parchment paper. On the baking sheet, spread out the yellow squash, red bell pepper, and chickpeas. Drizzle with olive oil, sprinkle with salt and pepper, and toss with your hands until evenly coated. Bake for 20 minutes. Remove from the oven and set aside to cool.

3. To a medium bowl, add the mixed salad greens, roasted veggies and chickpeas, pumpkin seeds, and alfalfa sprouts, and drizzle on the beet dressing. Give it a gentle toss and enjoy.

yogi macrobiotic salad

SERVES 5

Like yoga, this salad is inspired by staying grounded, practicing mindfulness, having inner peace, and maintaining unity of mind, body, and spirit. This salad is deeply nourishing and packed with anti-inflammatory, nutrient-dense plants. Make this salad for a more balanced, healthier you!

prep time:
15 minutes

cook time:
25 minutes

1 large sweet potato, peeled and cubed

1 large purple potato, cubed

1 (15oz/425g) can chickpeas, drained and rinsed

1 tbsp olive oil

Salt and ground black pepper, to taste

1 cup quinoa

½ tsp ground turmeric

2 cups shredded kale

1 cup shredded roasted seaweed

½ cup microgreens or sprouts

½ cup sauerkraut

1 tbsp hemp seeds

For the detox spirulina dressing (bonus dressing recipe!)

2 tbsp extra-virgin olive oil

3 tbsp tahini

Juice of 1 lemon

1 tbsp Dijon mustard

1 tsp garlic powder

½ tsp spirulina

Salt and ground black pepper, to taste

1. Preheat the oven to 425°F (220°C) and line a baking sheet with parchment paper.

2. To the lined baking sheet, add the sweet and purple potatoes and chickpeas. Drizzle on the olive oil and add salt and pepper to taste. Roast in the oven for 25 minutes or until potatoes are fork-tender. Set aside to cool.

3. While the potatoes and chickpeas bake, prepare the quinoa according to package instructions, adding the turmeric to the quinoa as it cooks. Set cooked quinoa aside to cool.

4. To a large bowl, add the shredded kale, seaweed, microgreens, sauerkraut, roasted potatoes and chickpeas, and cooked quinoa.

5. **Prepare the detox spirulina dressing** by whisking all the dressing ingredients in a small bowl or adding to a jar and shaking. Pour the dressing over top of the prepared salad. Garnish with hemp seeds, and enjoy!

Note

I like to use beet sauerkraut for this recipe, but any kind will work. Store any leftovers in an airtight container in the fridge for up to 3 days.

avocado "tuna" protein salad
(on toast)

SERVES 4–6

I freaking love a good tuna salad, and I've mastered the art of making a great plant-based tuna salad. This no-fish tuna salad is made with almonds and chickpeas, and it has avocado instead of mayo. This dish is packed with protein and is so versatile: enjoy on crackers or toast, with veggies, or on top of leafy greens. It doesn't get any easier than this no-mess food processor recipe!

prep time:
10 minutes

½ cup raw almonds

¼ cup chopped celery

⅓ cup roughly chopped white onion

¼ cup roughly chopped dill pickle

¼ block high-protein tofu

1 (15oz/425g) can chickpeas, rinsed and drained

1 medium avocado, pit and skin removed

¼ cup fresh dill

1 tbsp pickle brine

2 tbsp capers

1 tsp Dijon mustard

¼ cup shredded roasted nori

1 tsp salt

¼ tsp garlic powder

Pinch of ground black pepper

1 tbsp lemon (prevents browning, optional!)

1. To a food processor, add the almonds, celery, onion, and pickle. Pulse until combined but not turned to mush. Leave some texture.

2. Next, add the rest of the ingredients and pulse to combine well. Add the protein salad onto your favorite toast with anything from tomato slices or avocado slices to lettuce, or all of the above and more. I love to eat this with a crusty, thick sourdough!

wedgie veggie salad

SERVES 4–6

Wedge salads are something I used to only order at restaurants, but then I started making them at home, and it was a game changer. They're a simple-yet-different way to eat your typical salad. The coconut "bacon" is the best part, so don't skip it! Double the recipe if you're hosting a party and serve it on a large platter.

prep time:
10 minutes

cook time:
15 minutes

½ cup unsweetened coconut flakes

1 tbsp coconut aminos

½ tsp liquid smoke

1 tbsp maple syrup

¼ tsp salt

1 head iceberg lettuce, quartered

Dressing of your choice

1 cup halved cherry tomatoes

¼ cup diced chives

¼ cup diced red onion

Dressing options
- **Chipotle Ranch** (page 237)
- **Hemp Seed Caesar Dressing** (page 213)
- **ValleyGirl Ranch Dressing** (page 234)

1. **Make the coconut bacon.** In a medium nonstick pan over medium heat, add the coconut flakes and sauté for 4 minutes until toasty and golden. Add in the coconut aminos, liquid smoke, maple syrup, and salt. Mix well until evenly coated. Sauté for an additional 6 to 8 minutes, until crisp and golden, stirring continuously to avoid burning. Remove from the heat.

2. Transfer coconut bacon to a plate lined with paper towels so it stays crisp. Leave for 5 minutes.

3. **Assemble the salad.** On a large serving platter, arrange the quartered lettuce wedges. Top generously with the dressing of your choice. Then finish with the cherry tomatoes, chives, red onion, and coconut bacon. Enjoy!

hormone helper

SERVES 1

This salad is incredibly nourishing and works to support female hormones. The apple works wonders for balancing estrogen, while the fennel, which is rich in phytoestrogens and prebiotics, helps to gently balance hormones and support gut health. The vitamin C and fiber in the raw carrot are beneficial as well. Arugula gives the salad a peppery bite and is also great for thyroid health. This salad will be your new best friend—I like to eat this throughout the month, and it makes me feel amazing!

prep time:
10 minutes

1 large carrot, shaved into ribbons with vegetable peeler

1 cup arugula

½ cup thinly sliced fresh fennel bulb

½ red apple, thinly sliced

1 tbsp chopped walnuts

1 tbsp extra-virgin olive oil

Juice of ½ lemon

Salt and ground black pepper, to taste

Fresh dill

1. To a medium bowl, add the carrot ribbons, arugula, fennel slices, apple, walnuts, and olive oil. Squeeze the lemon juice over the top and add salt and freshly ground black pepper to taste. Toss until well combined.

2. Garnish with fresh dill, and enjoy immediately!

chopped kale + crispy tofu wrap

SERVES 2

This is probably my favorite way to eat a salad. Not only is it great for on-the-go convenience, but it's also a bit more filling because of the tortilla. Prep the tofu and salad the night before, then wrap it up the next day so it doesn't get soggy.

prep time:
20 minutes

cook time:
20 minutes

2 cups shredded kale

½ cup shredded carrots

½ cup thinly sliced red onion

1 cup cooked brown rice

1 batch **Chipotle Ranch** (page 237) or **Honeyless Mustard** (page 238)

2 large whole-wheat tortillas

For the crispy tofu tenders

½ cup chickpea flour

½ cup breadcrumbs

⅓ cup sesame seeds

½ tsp garlic powder

1 tsp salt

⅛ tsp ground black pepper

1 block extra-firm tofu, broken into 1 ½-in (3.8-cm) nuggets

Cooking oil spray

Note

Make sure you de-stem the kale before shredding the leaves. You can add a side of Chipotle Ranch for dipping.

---

1. **Make the crispy tofu tenders.** Preheat the air fryer or oven to 400°F (200°C). If using an oven, line a baking sheet with parchment paper.

2. In a shallow bowl, combine the chickpea flour with ¾ cup water, and mix well.

3. In another shallow bowl, add the breadcrumbs, sesame seeds, garlic powder, salt, and pepper. Stir together.

4. Dip each tofu nugget into the chickpea flour mixture and then roll in the breadcrumb mixture until completely coated. Gently place the breaded tofu either into the air fryer or onto the parchment-lined baking sheet. Spray the breaded nuggets with cooking oil.

5. Air-fry for 15 to 20 minutes or bake in the oven for 30 to 40 minutes, until golden brown. Set aside and allow to cool for about 15 minutes.

6. **Prepare the salad.** Into a large salad bowl, add the kale, carrots, onion, and cooked brown rice. Keep the tofu separate to retain its crispiness.

7. Drizzle on as much or as little Chipotle Ranch or Honeyless Mustard as you like, and toss well. Use a salad chopper, if you have one, to further chop the salad.

8. Assemble the wraps by placing a generous portion of the salad onto a large tortilla, add on the tofu, then roll it up, and enjoy!

fruit

SALADS

irresistibly refreshing

skin-glowing citrus avocado salad

SERVES 4

The vitamin C in the citrus combined with the healthy fats in the avocado make the perfect combination for glowing skin. Not only is it healthy, but it is also a gorgeous dish to serve to guests. You can also try sliced heirloom tomatoes instead of citrus, which makes for a delicious salad as well—it's a very versatile salad depending on what you have on hand.

prep time:
10 minutes

2 blood oranges

2 medium navel oranges

1 large grapefruit

2 large avocados, pit and skin removed, sliced

Juice of 1 lime

2 tbsp chopped fresh mint leaves

1 tbsp extra-virgin olive oil

Salt and ground black pepper, to taste

1. First, slice the oranges and grapefruits. Cut the top and bottom off each fruit. Stand them upright, then using a knife, cut the peel off. Cut each fruit into rounds, and remove any seeds you see.

2. On a platter, arrange the citrus and avocado slices. Squeeze the lime juice over the top of the salad, and sprinkle with chopped mint.

3. Drizzle with olive oil, and season with salt and pepper.

4. Serve fresh and enjoy.

digestion detox

SERVES 2–4

Healthy, regular digestion is key to good gut health. Eating fiber- and vitamin-rich fruit will keep your colon clean and your morning bathroom trips a little bit easier! To prevent constipation, eat this in the morning on an empty stomach with a glass of water (or warm lemon water). This is magical for the gut and works wonders. Happy gut, happy life!

prep time:
15 minutes

1 cup cubed papaya or cantaloupe

1 cup cubed pineapple

2 small kiwis, diced

1 large yellow dragon fruit, peeled and cubed, or 1 cup raspberries

Juice of ½ lime

Pinch of coconut flakes

1. To a medium bowl, add all the chopped fruit, then garnish with a squeeze of fresh lime juice and coconut flakes. Serve fresh.

Note

This salad stores well in an airtight container in the fridge for up to 2 days. Feel free to toast your coconut flakes for added flavor!

pretty in pink

SERVES 4–6

Sunday plan with a girlfriend: make this fruit salad, then take the salad and a bottle of our favorite sparkly drink to the park to have a little girls'-date picnic. Not only is this fruit salad pretty, but it's also packed with disease-fighting antioxidants. A little tip for washing your raspberries: rinse gently, then pat them dry with a clean kitchen towel so they don't get mushy.

prep time:
20 minutes

1 cup pitted fresh cherries

2 cups cubed watermelon

1 cup fresh raspberries

1 cup sliced fresh strawberries

½ cup pomegranate arils

1 large grapefruit, peeled and sliced

2 tbsp chopped fresh mint

Juice of ½ lime

1. In a large bowl, add all the ingredients. Mix gently, and enjoy fresh!

rainbow collagen booster

SERVES 2–3

Did you know that consuming vitamin C actually stimulates collagen production? This fruit salad is absolutely packed with vitamin C, one of the most important antioxidants you can consume. Eat this fruit salad to support glowing, plump, healthy, hydrated skin, and enjoy it first thing in the morning with herbal tea for additional digestive benefits. You can use any fruit you like or that is accessible to you in this dish. (The more colors, the greater the nutrients!)

prep time:
10 minutes

½ cup diced fresh strawberries

½ cup fresh raspberries

½ cup fresh blueberries

½ cup halved fresh golden berries (aka Cape gooseberry or ground-cherry)

2 clementines, peeled and segmented

1 cup cubed fresh pineapple

½ cup cubed fresh mango

½ cup chopped green apple

1 small kiwi, diced

Juice of 1 lime or juice of ½ orange, optional

1. To a medium bowl, add all the fruit and toss gently.

2. Squeeze fresh lime juice over the top if you want!

Note

Store any leftovers in an airtight container in the fridge for up to 3 days.

party parfait

A gorgeous layered parfait is a great breakfast option, but if you need to serve a large family or want to host a classy brunch, a big party parfait in a glass trifle bowl is the way to go. Don't let the beauty of this dish fool you—it's beyond easy to put together. If you're short on time, use store-bought granola.

prep time:
20 minutes

cook time:
20 minutes

⅓ cup maple syrup

¼ cup almond butter

¼ cup coconut oil or olive oil

2 cups organic gluten-free old-fashioned rolled oats

¼ cup pumpkin seeds

1 cup roughly chopped walnuts

Pinch of salt

64oz (907g) plain or coconut vegan yogurt

1 cup natural blueberry jam

2 cups fresh raspberries

2 cups fresh blueberries

1 cup fresh blackberries

1. Preheat the oven to 350°F (180°C). Line a baking sheet with parchment paper.

2. In a medium bowl, combine the maple syrup, almond butter, and coconut oil. Mix well. Add in the oats, pumpkin seeds, chopped walnuts, and salt. Mix again until well combined, then spread evenly onto the lined baking sheet.

3. Bake for 20 minutes, then set aside and let cool for 30 minutes.

4. In a trifle bowl, add about a third of the cooled granola to the bottom. Next layer the yogurt over the top, then the blueberry jam, then the berries. You can keep the berries separate or mix them together before layering. Continue to layer your ingredients until you've reached the top of the trifle bowl.

5. Serve and enjoy!

Note

I like to get natural blueberry jam without any sugar added, but go with your preference!

---

melon mama

SERVES 6

Melons are one of those hydrating fruits that deeply nourish the body. Melons like cantaloupe, watermelon, and honeydew help to boost the immune system; reduce the risk of heart attack; and support liver, kidney, and bowel health. Melons digest very quickly, so they are best eaten first thing in the morning on an empty stomach. You'll find glorious benefits for your gut health, including preventing constipation, when you wake up and eat this Melon Mama salad.

prep time:
15 minutes

1 baby watermelon, cubed or scooped using a melon baller

1 large cantaloupe, cubed or scooped using a melon baller

1 large honeydew, cubed or scooped using a melon baller

Juice of 1 lime

Freshly chopped mint

1. To a large bowl, combine all the cut melons, then add as much lime juice and freshly chopped mint as you like. Mix well to combine.

Note

Store any leftovers in an airtight container in the fridge for up to 3 days. If you have extra melon, freeze it and then make melon sorbet!

chopped cinnamon apple salad
(on pumpkin chia pudding)

SERVES 1

Make this easy, delicious breakfast the night before to set yourself up for success.
Make as much as 4 or 5 servings at a time for ready-to-go breakfasts all week long.

prep time:
5 minutes

chill time:
4 hours or
overnight

1 apple, chopped

1 tsp lemon juice

½ tsp ground cinnamon

1 tsp maple syrup

For the chia pudding

3 tbsp chia seeds

½ cup nondairy milk

1 tbsp maple syrup

2 tbsp canned pumpkin purée

1 tbsp almond butter

Optional toppings

Granola

Hemp seeds

Cinnamon

1. **Prepare the chia pudding.** In a small container or jar, mix together the chia pudding ingredients. Place in the refrigerator for at least 4 hours or overnight to chill and gel.

2. The next morning, **assemble the apple salad** by adding the chopped apple, lemon juice, cinnamon, and maple syrup to a small bowl. Mix well.

3. Serve the apple salad over the top of the chia pudding, then sprinkle with granola or hemp seeds and more cinnamon, if using, and enjoy!

sunshine bowl

SERVES 2

This is literally sunshine in a bowl. It looks happy; it makes you feel happy when you eat it; and it's filled with good-for-you ingredients that you need more of in your diet. Mango, kiwi, and cucumber are all hydrating and are great for supporting digestion, preventing constipation, boosting the immune system (thanks to the high vitamin C content), and promoting supple, plump, healthy skin.

prep time:
5 minutes

2 Champagne mangoes, peeled and cubed

1 cup diced cucumber

2 small kiwis, diced

2 tsp Tajín seasoning

1 tbsp lime juice

1 tsp agave syrup

1. To a large bowl, add all the ingredients.

2. Toss and enjoy!

Note

Eat fresh or store any leftovers in an airtight container in the fridge for up to 2 days.

blackberry + peach salad
(on whipped ricotta toast)

SERVES 3–4

This is a breakfast for when you don't have a busy day. Enjoy a slow, self-care morning. Do a little yoga, make this toast, read a good book, and enjoy every bite.

prep time:
20 minutes

cook time:
10 minutes

1 tbsp olive oil

2 slices sourdough bread (preferably long and thickly sliced)

1 pint blackberries

1–2 ripe fresh peaches, diced

1 tsp maple syrup

For the almond ricotta

1 cup skinless almonds

1 tsp lemon juice

½ tsp salt

½ tsp vanilla or the insides of 1 fresh vanilla bean

1 pitted Medjool date

⅓ cup nondairy milk

1. **Prepare the almond ricotta.** To a food processor, add all the almond ricotta ingredients and blend until smooth. Set aside.

2. In a large pan over medium-high heat, add the olive oil and the bread slices. Toast until both sides are golden brown.

3. To a medium bowl, add the blackberries, peaches, and maple syrup. Mix well.

4. Top the toast with the whipped almond ricotta and the peach salad. Yum!

Note

If you don't have a good quality food processor, soak the almonds for 1 hour in hot water before blending.

---

chunky monkey

SERVES 1

Breakfast doesn't get any easier than this. I love when a breakfast recipe is super nutrient-dense but also tastes like a treat at the same time.

prep time:
5 minutes

2 tbsp peanut butter

¼ cup plain vegan yogurt

1 tbsp soy milk

1 tbsp chocolate or vanilla protein powder, optional

1 banana, sliced

Optional toppings

Cacao nibs

Ground cinnamon

Granola

Hemp seeds

Chia seeds

Slivered almonds

Shredded coconut

1. In a small bowl, mix the peanut butter, yogurt, milk, and protein powder, if using.

2. Add the peanut butter protein yogurt to the plate, then top with bananas.

3. Garnish with any toppings you like—yum!

fruit salsa
(with cinnamon chips)

SERVES 4–6

If you love chips and salsa, then stop right here, because this version of chips and salsa is made with fruit instead of veggies, and the homemade chips taste like cinnamon churros. This is such a fun and easy snack idea for entertaining.

prep time:
25 minutes

cook time:
10 minutes

1 cup diced fresh strawberries

1 cup diced fresh nectarines

1 cup finely diced apple

1 cup diced fresh pineapple

1 cup diced watermelon

1 large mango, diced

2 small kiwis, diced

For the cinnamon chips

4 tortillas (whole wheat, wheat, or gluten-free)

1 tbsp melted coconut oil

1 tbsp maple syrup

1 tbsp ground cinnamon

1 tbsp coconut sugar

1. Preheat the oven to 350°F (180°C). Line two baking sheets with parchment paper.

2. **Make the cinnamon chips.** Cut the tortillas into triangles, then toss them in a medium bowl with the melted coconut oil, maple syrup, cinnamon, and coconut sugar. Spread the coated tortilla triangles evenly on the lined baking sheets. Bake for 10 minutes, then allow to cool for 10 additional minutes.

3. To a large bowl, add all the diced fruit. Dip the cinnamon chips into the fruit salsa, and enjoy, baby!

grain

SALADS

hearty grains of goodness in every bite

moroccan-inspired couscous salad

SERVES 4

This is one of my *all-time* favorite salads. Couscous, which is just small granules of semolina (durum wheat), is an underrated grain that can be used as a hearty base for any salad. If you are gluten-free, you can use quinoa as a substitute. The Moroccan seasoning blend is something I like to keep on hand because it goes well in salad dressings, on roasted veggies, in soups and stews, and more.

prep time:
10 minutes

cook time:
5 minutes

1 cup whole-wheat couscous

1½ cups chopped apple

½ cup golden raisins

½ cup sliced green olives

⅓ cup chopped pistachios

½ cup crumbled vegan feta cheese

1 cup finely chopped fresh parsley

½ cup finely chopped fresh mint

½ tsp salt

Pinch of ground black pepper

For the Moroccan seasoning blend

1 teaspoon ground cumin

1 teaspoon paprika

½ teaspoon ground cinnamon

½ teaspoon ground ginger

½ teaspoon ground coriander

¼ teaspoon ground turmeric

For the dressing

⅓ cup extra-virgin olive oil

¼ cup lemon juice

Moroccan seasoning blend

1. **Make the Moroccan seasoning blend.** In a small bowl, mix together the Moroccan seasoning blend ingredients, then set aside.

2. Cook the couscous according to package instructions.

3. **Prepare the salad.** To a large salad bowl, add the cooked couscous, apple, raisins, olives, pistachios, vegan feta, parsley, mint, salt, and pepper.

4. **Make the dressing.** In a small bowl, whisk together the dressing ingredients.

5. Pour the dressing over top of the salad. Mix well, and enjoy.

Note

Store any leftover Moroccan seasoning blend in an airtight container at room temperature for up to 1 year.

tuscan butter-bean salad

SERVES 4

Hearty, fresh, filling, savory, and beyond gorgeous—this takes butter-bean salads to the next level. If you haven't ever had butter beans, they are delicious, tender, super easy to find in any grocery store, and packed with plant protein and fiber. The sweet potato hummus combined with the couscous, beans, and nutty pesto will have your mouth watering.

prep time:
35 minutes

cook time:
40 minutes

1 cup pearled couscous

2 (15oz/425g) cans butter beans, rinsed and drained

1 batch **Walnutty Pesto Dressing** (page 230)

Juice of ½ lemon

Chopped fresh parsley

Salt and ground black pepper, to taste

For the sweet potato hummus

1 large sweet potato, cut in half lengthwise

1 (15oz/425g) can chickpeas, rinsed and drained

½ cup extra-virgin olive oil

¼ cup tahini

2 tbsp lemon juice

3 cloves garlic

2 tsp salt

1. Preheat the oven to 425°F (220°C). Line a baking sheet with parchment paper.

2. On the lined baking sheet, place the sweet potato with the flat sides down. Roast for 40 minutes or until fork-tender.

3. Cook the pearled couscous according to package instructions; 1 cup should yield about 2 cups of cooked pearled couscous. Set aside.

4. **Make the sweet potato hummus.** To a food processor, add the roasted sweet potatoes by scooping the flesh out of the skin, and the remaining sweet potato hummus ingredients. Blend until smooth.

5. In a serving dish, spread the sweet potato hummus on the bottom.

6. In a separate bowl, mix together the cooked pearled couscous, drained butter beans, and the Walnutty Pesto Dressing.

7. Top the sweet potato hummus with the butter bean and couscous salad.

8. Squeeze the fresh lemon juice over the top, and garnish with chopped fresh parsley. Season with salt and pepper to taste.

are you figgin' kidding me?

SERVES 4

Fresh figs are absolutely delicious in salads, and this one really is figgin' amazing. The combination of the sweet and crunchy candied nuts, the fresh and juicy figs, and the savory roasted vegetables makes for a satiating salad that you'll be obsessed with.

prep time:
20 minutes

cook time:
35 minutes

½ cup wild rice

1 cup arugula or spinach

2 cups spring mix

5 fresh figs, quartered

¼ cup chopped pistachios

Handful of vegan cheese crumbles (vegan goat, feta, or Parmesan are great options)

1 batch **Balsamic Baby** dressing (page 225)

For the roasted vegetables

1 medium sweet potato, peeled and cubed

2 cups quartered Brussels sprouts

2 tbsp olive oil

¼ tsp garlic powder

1 tsp salt

¼ tsp ground black pepper

For the candied pecans

1 cup raw pecans

2 tbsp maple syrup

1 tbsp melted coconut oil

¼ tsp salt

1. **Roast the vegetables.** Preheat the oven to 400°F (200°C). Line two baking sheets with parchment paper.

2. To one lined baking sheet, add the sweet potato cubes and Brussels sprouts. Be sure to spread them evenly. Season with the olive oil, garlic powder, salt, and pepper. Mix well. Roast the potatoes in the oven for 25 to 35 minutes or until golden brown and fork-tender.

3. **Make the candied pecans.** In a small bowl, combine the raw pecans, maple syrup, melted coconut oil, and salt. To the second lined baking sheet, add the pecan mixture, and in the last 10 minutes of the potatoes roasting, add the candied pecans to the oven. Remove both potatoes and pecans from the oven and allow to cool for 10 minutes.

4. **Cook the wild rice** according to package instructions. Fluff with a fork and set aside.

5. **Assemble the salad.** In a large salad bowl or platter, add the cooked wild rice, arugula, spring mix, and roasted sweet potatoes and Brussels sprouts. Place the quartered figs over the salad, and top with chopped pistachios, vegan cheese, and candied pecans. Drizzle with the Balsamic Baby dressing, and enjoy!

healthy goddess orzo

SERVES 4–6

It's pretty, it's pink; it's filled with greens, creamy avocado, and nutritious microgreens, and it contains arguably one of the best inventions: orzo. This salad is not only gorgeous and colorful, but it also makes you feel great! It provides vitamins and energy, and it's super easy to make. I love hosting a few girlfriends for dinner and making this for everyone with a side of grilled tofu and mocktails—it's always a hit.

prep time:
15 minutes

cook time:
10 minutes

16oz (450g) orzo

2 cups chopped baby spinach

1 cup diced strawberries

1 large avocado, pit and skin removed, diced

½ cup thinly sliced red onion

1 cup shredded radicchio leaves

½ cup thinly sliced radishes (see note)

¼ cup microgreens

1 tbsp chopped fresh mint

¼ cup chopped fresh dill

¾ cup crumbled vegan feta

1 tbsp extra-virgin olive oil

1 tsp salt

Freshly ground black pepper

2 batches **Raspberry Vinaigrette** (page 198)

1. Boil water and cook the orzo according to package instructions. Set aside to cool.

2. While the orzo cooks, prepare the veggies.

3. To a large salad bowl, add all the ingredients. Pour the dressing over top, toss, and enjoy!

> **Note**
> I like to use a combination of watermelon radish and regular radish in this recipe. You may want to soak the sliced red onions in cold water to get rid of any bitterness.

golden goddess salad

SERVES 6–8

This anti-inflammatory, nutrient-packed quinoa-based salad is full of those good-for-you red and yellow veggies that help to regulate the nervous system, prevent heart disease, and even support eye health. This is another one of those salads that holds up nicely in the fridge for lunches all week long. Don't like quinoa? You can use anything for the base from wild rice to whole-wheat orzo.

prep time:
15 minutes

cook time:
25 minutes

1 large sweet potato, peeled and cubed

2 cups diced carrots

1 large yellow squash, diced

1 large orange bell pepper, ribs and seeds removed, diced

1 large yellow bell pepper, ribs and seeds removed, diced

2 ears corn, kernels cut off cob

2 tbsp olive oil

1 tsp salt

½ tsp ground black pepper

½ tsp garlic powder

4 cups cooked white quinoa with turmeric (see note)

1 (15oz/425g) can chickpeas, rinsed and drained

1 batch **Golden Goddess Sunshine Dressing** (page 241)

1. Preheat the oven to 425°F (220°C). Line a large baking sheet with parchment paper.

2. Place the sweet potato, carrots, squash, bell peppers, and corn onto the prepared baking sheet. Drizzle with olive oil and season with salt, pepper, and garlic powder, then toss to coat well. Roast for 25 minutes or until the sweet potatoes are tender. Remove from the oven.

3. In a large bowl, toss the cooked quinoa, roasted veggies, and chickpeas with the Golden Goddess Sunshine Dressing until well combined.

4. Enjoy! Store leftovers in an airtight container in the fridge for up to 4 days.

Note

When cooking the quinoa according to package instructions, add a ½ tsp of ground turmeric to the cooking water for a flavor and antioxidant boost.

wild rice salad

SERVES 4

Every time I make this salad for a friend or guest, they always ask for the recipe. I think it's the sweet-and-savory combination that is scrumptious in a salad. The apple, dried cherries, onion, and wild rice all work so well together. I like to make this in the fall with a big pot of soup and some good, crusty bread on the side.

prep time:
15 minutes

cook time:
30 minutes

2 cups sliced carrot

1 large fresh beet, peeled and chopped

1 cup sliced leeks

1 tbsp olive oil

1 tbsp maple syrup

¼ tsp garlic powder

1 tsp salt

¼ tsp ground black pepper

3 cups fresh spinach leaves

1 cup cooked wild rice

1 Honeycrisp apple, diced

½ cup sliced red onion

¼ cup dried cherries or dried cranberries

⅓ cup slivered almonds

Dressing options

· **30-Second Red Wine Vinaigrette** (page 197)

· **Balsamic Baby** (page 225)

· **Balsamic Tahini Dressing** (page 245)

1. Preheat oven to 400°F (200°C). Line a baking sheet with parchment paper.

2. To the lined baking sheet, add the carrot, beet, and leeks. Season with olive oil, maple syrup, garlic powder, salt, and pepper. Roast in the oven until the carrots are tender, about 30 minutes.

3. To a large salad bowl, add the spinach, cooked wild rice, and roasted veggies straight from the oven. Toss together to wilt the spinach slightly.

4. Add the apple, red onion, dried cherries, and almonds. Toss with the dressing of your choice, and enjoy!

superfood brain-booster salad

SERVES 2

Eating food that fuels and nourishes your brain is super important. For example, foods rich in omega-3 fatty acids and other healthy fats, like walnuts and avocado, as well as fruit filled with antioxidants, like blueberries and mango, help to prevent neurological decline. I wanted to develop a salad that is perfectly crafted to support brain health. Eat as much of this Superfood Brain-Booster Salad as you can squeeze in—your brain will thank you for it.

prep time:
10 minutes

cook time:
15 minutes

3 cups baby spinach

1 cup fresh blueberries

¼ cup chopped walnuts

2 tbsp slivered almonds

1½ cups cooked quinoa

1 large avocado, pit and skin removed, diced

1 large red bell pepper, ribs and seeds removed, diced

1 large mango, diced

Dressing options

- **Balsamic Tahini Dressing** (page 245)
- Balsamic vinegar and extra-virgin olive oil
- **Perfect Poppy Seed Dressing** (page 217)
- **Raspberry Vinaigrette** (page 198)

1. To a large salad bowl, add all the ingredients.

2. Drizzle with the dressing of your choice, and toss to combine.

adzuki bean salad

SERVES 4–6

I love the Whole Foods Market hot bar. They have this incredible adzuki miso bean salad that is *delicious*, but I noticed the ingredients weren't up to my standards. I thought I could make this at home with better-for-you ingredients and for less money, so I developed this recipe and wow—it doesn't disappoint. It's savory, crunchy, hearty, and packed with protein and fiber. Can't find adzuki beans? Use black beans instead.

prep time:
10 minutes

cook time:
25 minutes

1 large sweet potato, peeled and cubed

2 tbsp olive oil or avocado oil

Salt and ground black pepper, to taste

1 cup farro

1 cup diced purple cabbage

1 (15oz/425g) can adzuki beans, rinsed and drained

1 cup shredded carrots

1 cup edamame, de-shelled and steamed

⅓ cup chopped roasted cashews

½ cup chopped cilantro

1 batch **Creamy Dreamy Peanut Dressing** (page 214)

⅓ cup sliced green onions

1. Preheat the oven to 400°F (200°C). Line a baking sheet with parchment paper.

2. To the lined baking sheet, add the sweet potato cubes, then drizzle with olive oil and mix to evenly coat. Season with salt and pepper to taste.

3. Roast in the oven for 25 minutes or until the sweet potatoes are golden and fork-tender.

4. Make the farro according to the bag instructions.

5. To a large bowl, add the cooked farro, cabbage, beans, carrots, edamame, cashews, cilantro, and dressing. Toss the salad. Top with sliced green onions as garnish, and enjoy!

gut-loving farro salad

SERVES 4–6

Farro is one of those underused, underrated whole grains that should be in everyone's pantry as a plant-based staple. I like to describe farro as if barley and rice had a baby. It's super simple to make—just boil it until it's tender, like you would pasta. I like to make it and toss it with delicious freshly roasted vegetables, protein- and fiber-packed lentils, and a Balsamic Tahini Dressing that's to die for.

prep time:
10 minutes

cook time:
25 minutes

2 red bell peppers, ribs and seeds removed, chopped

2 ears corn, kernels cut off cob

1 red onion, chopped

8 cloves garlic, minced

1 large zucchini, cubed

2 tbsp olive oil

Salt and ground black pepper, to taste

1 cup farro

1 cup brown lentils

1 batch **Balsamic Tahini Dressing** (page 245)

Fresh basil leaves

½ cup sliced Italian green olives

½ cup crumbled vegan feta, optional

1. Preheat the oven to 425°F (220°C), and line two baking sheets with parchment paper.

2. To the lined baking sheets, add the bell peppers, corn, red onion, garlic, and zucchini. Split the veggies up amongst both lined sheets. Drizzle with olive oil, and season with salt and pepper to taste. Mix well to evenly coat all ingredients with oil. Roast for 25 minutes.

3. While the vegetables roast, cook the farro and brown lentils according to package directions for each. Set aside to cool.

4. To a large bowl, add the roasted veggies, cooked farro, cooked lentils, and Balsamic Tahini Dressing (as much or as little dressing as you'd like). Toss to combine, then top with fresh basil, sliced green olives, and vegan feta, if using. Enjoy!

pasta

SALADS

what could be a better combination?

spring roll salad

SERVES 8

Do you love spring rolls but are too lazy to roll them in rice paper? Meet the spring roll salad: a deconstructed spring roll in a bowl. It didn't go viral on Instagram for nothing—16 million people from around the world saw my video! From the noodles and the crispy veggies to the crunchy nuts and Creamy Dreamy Peanut Dressing, you are going to be addicted to this salad.

prep time:
20 minutes

cook time:
5 minutes

12oz (340g) thin rice noodles

1 large cucumber, julienned

1 cup thinly sliced cabbage

2 large carrots, julienned

1 large red bell pepper, ribs and seeds removed, thinly sliced

¼ cup chopped roasted peanuts

⅓ cup chopped fresh cilantro

¼ cup sliced green onion

2 batches **Creamy Dreamy Peanut Dressing** (page 214)

2 tsp sesame seeds

1. Cook the rice noodles according to package instructions. Rinse with cold water, drain, and place in a large bowl.

2. To the large bowl, add the cucumber, cabbage, carrots, bell pepper, peanuts, cilantro, and green onion. Pour the dressing over top (as little or as much as you'd like). Toss with tongs, garnish with sesame seeds, and serve!

> **Note**
> This stores well in an airtight container in the fridge for up to 3 days. Do not heat the leftovers; instead, eat it cold.

caesar pasta salad

SERVES 4

This salad is the marriage of arguably two of the best foods our world has to offer: Caesar salad and pasta. Adding pasta to a Caesar salad makes it hearty, filling, and beyond delish. Use any pasta you like, from penne to rotini. You can use whole-wheat pasta or even a high-protein alternative, like chickpea-based pasta. Are you gluten-free? Use GF pasta!

prep time:
10 minutes

cook time:
15 minutes

8oz (225g) pasta of your choice

1 block high-protein or extra firm tofu

1 tbsp olive oil

Salt, to taste

1 head dinosaur kale, chopped

1 pint halved cherry tomatoes

½ cup shaved vegan Parmesan

1 batch **Hemp Seed Caesar Dressing** (page 213)

1. Cook the pasta according to package instructions. Rinse with cold water, drain, and set aside.

2. Break the tofu into 1-inch bite-size pieces. In a large nonstick skillet over medium-high heat, heat the olive oil and sauté the tofu pieces until they are golden brown on both sides. Salt the tofu to taste. Alternatively, you can grill the tofu on an indoor panini press.

3. To a large bowl, add the cooked pasta, cooked tofu, kale, tomatoes, and shaved Parmesan. Pour the Hemp Seed Caesar Dressing over the top (as much or as little as you want), then toss and enjoy!

the italian

SERVES 6

Now this is a salad I could eat every single day, because it is such a classic combination. It's fresh, perfect for easy grab-and-go lunches, and stores great in the fridge. I highly recommend making a big batch and dividing it into 4 to 6 airtight containers for meal prep to bring to work or school. Make it for a birthday lunch, or bring it to a potluck or book club meeting. This will be a fridge staple!

prep time:
5 minutes

cook time:
10 minutes

16oz (450g) rotini

1 (15oz/425g) can chickpeas, drained and rinsed

2 cups halved cherry tomatoes

1 (12 oz) jar roasted red peppers, chopped

1 (12 oz) jar pickled and sliced banana peppers

½ cup sliced red onion

½ cup sliced black olives

1 cup chopped marinated artichoke hearts

1 batch **ItalianGirl Dressing** (page 218)

1. Cook the pasta according to package instructions. Rinse in cold water and drain.

2. To a large salad bowl, add the cooked pasta, chickpeas, tomatoes, roasted red peppers, banana peppers, onion, olives, and artichoke hearts.

3. Toss with the ItalianGirl Dressing, and enjoy!

soba noodle salad
(with sesame-crunch tofu)

SERVES 3

If you want the ultimate complete plant-based meal, this delicious and fresh Soba Noodle Salad is the best complement to my signature crispy sesame-crunch tofu. It's also a great way to sneak in veggies like mushrooms and asparagus!

prep time:
30 minutes

cook time:
20 minutes

1 tbsp avocado oil or sesame oil

3 cloves garlic, minced

20 asparagus spears, chopped diagonally

2 cups sliced shiitake mushrooms

1 large zucchini, julienned

2 cups chopped spinach

1 tbsp tahini

1 tbsp rice vinegar

1 tsp mirin

1 tbsp sriracha

3 tbsp soy sauce

1 tsp red or white miso paste

1 tbsp toasted sesame oil

8oz (225g) fresh soba noodles

Sliced green onions

For the sesame-crunch tofu

¼ cup unsweetened soy milk

1 tsp apple cider vinegar

¼ cup chickpea flour

1 cup breadcrumbs or ground crackers

¼ cup toasted sesame seeds

¼ tsp garlic powder

¼ tsp salt

1 block high-protein tofu, sliced into 4–5 filets

Cooking oil spray

1. **Make the sesame-crunch tofu.** Preheat the oven or an air fryer to 400°F (200°C). Line a baking sheet with parchment paper if baking in the oven.

2. To a wide, shallow bowl, add the soy milk, apple cider vinegar, and chickpea flour. Mix until a batter forms.

3. In a second wide, shallow bowl, add the breadcrumbs, sesame seeds, garlic powder, and salt.

4. Dip each tofu filet into the batter, then into the breadcrumb mixture, making sure to coat evenly. Place each filet on the lined baking sheet. Spray the filets with cooking oil spray. (I like to use olive oil).

5. Bake or air-fry until golden brown on both sides, flipping once, about 10 to 15 minutes on each side in the oven and 15 minutes total in an air fryer. Set aside.

6. **Make the noodle salad.** To a large nonstick pan set over medium-high heat, add the avocado oil and garlic. Sauté for 1 minute. Add the asparagus, mushrooms, and zucchini. Sauté for about 5 minutes or until tender but still vibrant and not mushy. Add in the spinach and remove from heat. Set aside.

7. In a small bowl, add the tahini, rice vinegar, mirin, sriracha, soy sauce, miso paste, and sesame oil. Whisk the sauce well to combine. Set aside.

8. Rinse the soba noodles with cold water, then add to a large salad bowl with the sautéed veggies. Pour the sauce over top and toss with tongs.

9. On a plate or in a bowl, serve the noodles topped with a crunchy sesame tofu filet and garnished with green onions. Enjoy!

"tuna" pasta salad

SERVES 8–10

This is basically happiness in a bowl and is the true ideal salad. It has pasta in it—which we're all happy about—the dressing is creamy and easy to make, the veggies are all crunchy and fresh, and the chickpeas make for a great tuna-like texture and protein alternative. If there's one salad you're going to be repeating for meal-prep lunches, it's this one.

prep time:
20 minutes

cook time:
10 minutes

16oz (340g) macaroni

1 (15oz/425g) can chickpeas, drained and rinsed

1 cup diced celery

1 large red bell pepper, ribs and seeds removed, diced

½ cup diced red onion

1 cup steamed green peas

3 tbsp chopped fresh dill

For the dressing

½ cup plain vegan yogurt

½ cup vegan mayonnaise

¼ cup pickle brine

2 tsp lemon juice

1 tbsp Dijon mustard

2 tsp salt

½ tsp ground black pepper

1 tsp garlic powder

1. Cook the macaroni according to package instructions. Rinse with cold water, drain, and set aside.

2. **Make the dressing.** In a medium bowl, add all the dressing ingredients, and whisk together until combined.

3. In a large salad bowl, add the chickpeas and mash with a potato masher or a fork until smooth.

4. To the salad bowl, add the cooked macaroni, veggies, and dressing. Stir until everything is well coated in the dressing. Enjoy!

avocado dream pasta

SERVES 6

Creamy dreamy avocado pesto pasta is not only delicious, but it's also good for your hair, skin, nails, and hormones. Did you know avocados can help lower LDL (bad cholesterol) and increase HDL (good cholesterol)? Avocados are packed with folate; magnesium; potassium (even more than bananas); fiber; vitamins C, E, and K; and more. Moral of the story: add avocados to your pasta sauces for amazing nutritional benefits.

prep time:
10 minutes

cook time:
10 minutes

16oz (450g) pasta of your choice

1 large ripe avocado, pit and skin removed

⅓ cup extra-virgin olive oil

2½ cups fresh basil leaves

1 cup baby spinach

3 tbsp lemon juice

½ cup hemp seeds

4 cloves garlic

1 tbsp nutritional yeast

1 tsp salt

Pinch of ground black pepper

Optional garnishes

Red pepper flakes

Freshly ground black pepper

Lemon juice

Vegan Parmesan

Extra-virgin olive oil

1. Begin cooking the pasta according to package instructions. Save 1 cup of the pasta water.

2. While the pasta cooks, to a blender or food processor, add the rest of the ingredients and blend on high to create the sauce.

3. Once the pasta is done cooking, drain, transfer to a serving bowl, and pour the sauce over top. Add the pasta water and toss until the pasta is well coated.

4. Garnish with anything your heart desires, and enjoy fresh and warm!

plant-goddess tortellini
(with walnutty pesto)

SERVES 6

Tortellini combined with homemade Walnutty Pesto Dressing and veggies makes for a perfect dish to bring to a girls' lunch or to meal-prep for your own lunch. This dish is just as good the next day—which we love. I use store-bought dairy-free tortellini, but if you can't find it in a store near you, feel free to use any pasta you want. Penne is a great alternative.

prep time:
15 minutes

cook time:
10 minutes

16oz (450g) tortellini

1 tbsp olive oil

2 cups chopped broccoli

Salt and ground black pepper, to taste

2 cups halved cherry tomatoes

¾ cup chopped sun-dried tomatoes

1 cup sliced kalamata olives

½ cup chopped marinated artichoke hearts

1 batch **Walnutty Pesto Dressing** (page 230)

Fresh basil

1. Cook the tortellini according to package instructions. Rinse with cold water, drain, and set aside.

2. In a medium pan over medium-high heat, add the olive oil and sauté the broccoli for about 5 minutes until tender but not mushy. Add salt and pepper to taste.

3. To a large salad bowl, combine the cooked tortellini, sautéed broccoli, tomatoes, olives, and artichoke hearts.

4. Pour the Walnutty Pesto Dressing over top of the salad. Toss well to combine, garnish with fresh basil, and enjoy.

> **Note**
> Store leftovers in an airtight container in the fridge for up to 4 days.

summer elote pasta salad

SERVES 6–8

I swear—corn and pasta need to be paired together more often. The crunchy sweet
corn is the best complement to carby pasta. Of course, I had to create a vegan
Elote Dressing that is creamy, smoky, and flavorful, but completely dairy-free.
I love that this salad has only a few simple ingredients.

prep time:
15 minutes

cook time:
15 minutes

16oz (450g) campanelle pasta

3 ears corn, husks and silk
removed

1 batch **Elote Dressing** (page
233)

⅓ cup chopped cilantro

½ cup vegan feta

Salt and ground black pepper,
to taste

1. Bring a large pot of salted water to a boil.
   Cook the pasta according to package
   instructions. Rinse with cold water, drain,
   and set aside.

2. Preheat the oven to 450°F (230°C). Line a
   baking sheet with parchment paper.

3. On the lined baking sheet, place the ears of
   corn. Put in the oven and roast until all sides
   are charred, about 15 minutes, making sure
   to turn the corn every 5 minutes. Let cool
   and then cut the roasted corn off the cobs.
   Discard the cobs and set the corn aside.

4. To a large salad bowl, add the cooked pasta
   and Elote Dressing. Mix well to evenly coat
   the pasta.

5. Add the roasted corn, cilantro, and vegan
   feta to the bowl. Toss again gently.

6. Season with salt and pepper to taste
   if needed. Enjoy!

chipotle chica salad

SERVES 4

This is a shovel-in-your-mouth kind of pasta dish. No, really—when I was done taking pictures of this beauty, I grabbed a huge spoon and went to town. The creamy Chipotle Ranch is what makes this so freaking good. The roasted bell peppers and roasted corn give a hint of sweetness while the dressing makes this spicy and comforting. I like to add black beans to this dish, and you can even use protein pasta to sneak in some extra plant protein.

prep time:
10 minutes

cook time:
25 minutes

2 ears corn, husks and silk removed

2 red bell peppers, ribs and seeds removed, roughly diced

Cooking oil spray

Salt and ground black pepper, to taste

8oz (225g) shell pasta

1 (14oz/397g) can black beans, drained and rinsed

1 batch **Chipotle Ranch** (page 237)

¼ cup chopped fresh cilantro

1 lime, cut into wedges

1. Preheat the oven to 425°F (220°C). Line a baking sheet with parchment paper.

2. On the lined baking sheet, spread out the ears of corn and bell peppers. Spray with cooking oil spray (I like to use olive oil spray), and season with salt and pepper. Bake for 25 minutes, until slightly charred and tender, rotating the corn halfway. Once cooked, let cool slightly, and cut the corn off the cob. Discard the cobs and set the corn and bell peppers aside.

3. While the corn and peppers roast, boil a pot of water and cook the shells according to package instructions. Rinse with cold water, drain, and set aside.

4. To a large salad bowl, add the roasted corn, bell peppers, cooked pasta, and black beans.

5. Pour as much or as little dressing as you want over top. Mix well to combine, then garnish with cilantro. Serve with lime wedges.

Note

Store in the fridge in an airtight container for up to 3 days for optimal freshness.

---

chopped

SALADS

because chopped salads are superior

bbq tofu chopped salad

SERVES 4

Now this is a damn good salad. The richness of the ranch pairs perfectly with the tanginess of the barbecue sauce, and the crisp lettuce, creamy avocado, and sweetness of the corn are the best complements for the salad. Whip this dish up to serve at a family gathering, a summer picnic, or a potluck—everyone will love you for it.

prep time:
15 minutes

cook time:
10 minutes

1 tbsp olive oil

1 block high-protein tofu, dried and cut into bite-size pieces (see note)

Salt and ground black pepper, to taste

½ cup barbecue sauce

1 large head romaine lettuce, chopped

1 can black beans, drained and rinsed

1 cup halved cherry tomatoes

½ cup diced red onion

1 large avocado, diced

1 cup steamed or grilled corn

1 batch **ValleyGirl Ranch Dressing** (page 234)

1. To a medium pan over medium-high heat, add the olive oil and tofu pieces. Stir every few minutes until the tofu is golden brown on all sides, about 10 minutes. Season with salt and pepper to taste. Reduce the heat to a simmer and pour in the barbecue sauce. Stir until it thickens, then remove the pan from the heat and set aside to fully cool.

2. To a large salad bowl, add the lettuce, black beans, cherry tomatoes, red onion, avocado, and corn.

3. Once the tofu has cooled, add the tofu and sauce to the salad. Drizzle as much of the ValleyGirl Ranch Dressing as you like over top. Add additional barbecue sauce, if desired. Toss to combine, then enjoy fresh.

Note

Before cutting the tofu into bite-size pieces, remove as much of the moisture from it as possible. With a clean kitchen towel, simply pat the block of tofu dry. You can even put a heavy plate on top of it to force more of the moisture out.

green vibes–only salad

SERVES 4–6

Crunchy, crispy, stays fresh in the fridge for days, and tastes even better as leftovers: meet the Green Vibes–Only Salad. This dish is loaded with all kinds of nutrient-dense green veggies that we all forget to eat. Not only is this salad chopped and delicious, but it also won't get soggy in the fridge. I like to meal prep this salad along with rice and tofu for easy lunches during the week.

prep time:
20 minutes

cook time:
3 minutes

2 cups chopped dinosaur kale

2 tsp extra-virgin olive oil

1 cup edamame, steamed and de-shelled

2 cups chopped green cabbage

1 cup finely chopped broccoli

1 cup diced cucumber

1 avocado, pit and skin removed, diced

¼ cup sliced green onions

⅓ cup roasted salted pumpkin seeds

1 batch **Green Goodness Dressing** (page 242)

1. To a large bowl, add the kale and olive oil. With clean hands, massage the kale and oil together to make it less chewy.

2. To the bowl with the kale, add the edamame, green cabbage, broccoli, cucumber, avocado, and green onions, then sprinkle pumpkin seeds over the top.

3. Drizzle with the Green Goodness Dressing and toss to combine. Enjoy!

> **Note**
> Store in the fridge in an airtight container for up to 4 days.

chopped salad pita

SERVES 2

What's better than eating a chopped salad? I'll give you a hint: stuff your chopped salad into a pita pocket for the yummiest lunch. Use any pita you like, whether it's whole-wheat, wheat, or gluten-free.

prep time:
10 minutes

2 cups finely diced green-leaf lettuce

1 avocado, pit and skin removed, finely diced

2 Persian cucumbers, finely diced

¼ cup finely diced red onion

3 tbsp crumbled vegan feta

½ cup canned chickpeas, drained and rinsed

2 tbsp finely chopped dill

1 batch **Mediterranean Mama Dressing** (page 206)

2 pitas

1. To a medium salad bowl, add all the ingredients (except for the pita), using as little or as much of the dressing as you'd like. Toss to combine.

2. Stuff a generous portion of the salad into your pita pockets, and eat up.

vegan cobb salad

SERVES 6–8

A Cobb salad is a classic American salad. Traditionally, you'll find a Cobb salad packed with hard-boiled eggs, bacon, and blue cheese. My plant-based version of this beloved salad includes a smoky, sweet tempeh bacon, chickpeas, and vegan feta. Serve this as part of a buffet at a party and lay the ingredients out in neat rows so everyone can pick what they like.

prep time:
20 minutes

cook time:
10 minutes

2 heads romaine lettuce, chopped

2 cups halved cherry tomatoes

1 ripe avocado, pit and skin removed, cubed

1 cup steamed corn, cooled

½ cup thinly sliced red onion

¼ cup roasted salted sunflower seeds

1 (15oz/425g) can chickpeas, drained and rinsed

¾ cup vegan feta

2 batches **30-Second Red Wine Vinaigrette** (page 197)

2 tbsp chopped fresh chives

Salt and freshly ground black pepper, to taste

For the tempeh bacon

1 tbsp olive oil

1 (8oz/225g) package of tempeh, cut into bite-size pieces

3 tbsp coconut aminos

1 tsp liquid smoke

1 tbsp maple syrup

Pinch of garlic powder

1. **Make the tempeh bacon.** To a large nonstick pan over medium-high heat, add the olive oil and tempeh pieces, and sauté for about 5 minutes or until golden brown. While the tempeh cooks, to a small bowl, add the coconut aminos, liquid smoke, maple syrup, and garlic powder. Whisk to combine.

2. Reduce the heat to low and pour the sauce into the pan with the tempeh, stirring constantly until the sauce thickens, about 3 minutes. Remove from the heat and set aside. Allow tempeh to absorb the sauce for 5 minutes.

3. **Assemble the salad.** To the bottom of a large serving platter, add the chopped romaine lettuce.

4. In neat rows over top of the lettuce, add the tempeh bacon, cherry tomatoes, avocado, corn, red onion, sunflower seeds, chickpeas, and vegan feta.

5. Drizzle the 30-Second Red Wine Vinaigrette over top of the salad, and season with chopped chives, salt, and pepper. Enjoy!

Note

Squeeze lemon on the avocado to keep it from browning.

---

vegan waldorf salad

SERVES 3

There's something about the sweetness and crunchiness of a Waldorf salad that hits the spot. While there are so many different versions of this classic, I of course had to provide you with the secret to making it dairy-free. Using vegan yogurt means you can mimic a classic Waldorf salad dressing perfectly.

prep time:
10 minutes

cook time:
5 minutes

½ cup walnuts

1 head romaine lettuce, chopped

1 cup halved red seedless grapes

1 cup diced celery

1 large Granny Smith apple, diced

2 tbsp extra-virgin olive oil

3 tbsp plain vegan yogurt

½ tsp Dijon mustard

1 tbsp maple syrup

1 tbsp apple cider vinegar

½ tsp salt

Pinch of ground black pepper

1. In a medium nonstick pan, toast the walnuts on medium-high heat for 5 minutes, stirring every few seconds to prevent burning.

2. To a large salad bowl, add the romaine lettuce, grapes, celery, apple, and walnuts.

3. In a small bowl, whisk together the olive oil, vegan yogurt, mustard, maple syrup, apple cider vinegar, salt, and pepper. Pour over the salad and toss. Yummy, baby!

health-nut salad

SERVES 2

This salad is for the serious health nuts. It has all the good-for-you greens, cruciferous vegetables, healthy fats, and antioxidants. The salad bark on top is something you can make in advance and use as a salad topping all week long. Think of the salad bark as homemade seedy croutons that are packed with omega-3s.

prep time:
10 minutes

cook time:
60 minutes

2 cups shredded purple kale

1 cup raw chopped broccoli

1 cup chopped apple

1 cup shredded carrots

1 avocado, pit and skin removed, diced

For the salad bark

1 cup organic pumpkin seeds

⅓ cup sunflower seeds

1 cup whole flaxseed

⅓ cup sesame seeds

2 tbsp psyllium husk (or ground flaxseed)

1 tsp salt

Everything bagel seasoning, optional

Dressing options

- **30-Second Red Wine Vinaigrette** (page 197)
- **Balsamic Tahini Dressing** (page 245)
- **Mediterranean Mama Dressing** (page 206)

1. **Make the salad bark.** Preheat the oven to 325°F (160°C). Line a baking sheet with parchment paper.

2. In a large bowl, mix together the pumpkin seeds, sunflower seeds, whole flaxseed, sesame seeds, psyllium husk, and salt. Pour in 1½ cups boiling water and mix until combined.

3. To the lined baking sheet, add the seed mixture, and spread it out as evenly and thinly as possible. Top with everything bagel seasoning for extra flavor, if using.

4. Bake for 50 to 60 minutes, until crispy. Let cool for an hour, then break apart into 1-inch pieces and set aside.

5. **Prepare the salad.** To a salad bowl, add all the salad ingredients. Drizzle with the dressing of your choice and add some salad bark over the top. Enjoy!

> **Note**
>
> Keep any extra salad bark in an airtight container at room temperature for up to 7 days for salads throughout the week. The salad bark will crisp up as it cools!

pizza night salad

SERVES 6

Everyone loves a good pizza night. In our family, we like to make our own, and I *always* make this salad to go with our pizza. It's the perfect complement because it's salty, crunchy, fresh, healthy, easy to make, and great with pizza.

prep time:
20 minutes

1 head iceberg lettuce, shredded

1 cup shredded radicchio

½ cup halved cherry tomatoes

1 (15oz/425g) can chickpeas, drained and rinsed

1 cup sliced pepperoncini

½ cup sliced green olives

½ red onion, thinly sliced or diced

Vegan mozzarella, optional

Dressing options

- **30-Second Red Wine Vinaigrette** (page 197)
- **ItalianGirl Dressing** (page 218)

1. To a large salad bowl, add all the ingredients, including vegan mozzarella, if using. Toss with your dressing of choice, and enjoy.

Note

I like to use vegan cashew mozzarella to top my salad!

busygirl brussels salad

SERVES 3

This salad is for the busiest of bees. I like this one because you can make it on a Sunday and enjoy it for a few lunches in the days to come. With kale and Brussels sprouts as the base, it keeps well in the fridge. And the best part: this salad comes together in under 20 minutes!

prep time:
15 minutes

cook time:
1 minute

½ cup sliced red onion

2 tbsp apple cider vinegar

1 (15oz/425g) can chickpeas, drained and rinsed

1 tsp extra-virgin olive oil

1 tsp smoked paprika

¼ tsp salt

¼ tsp ground black pepper

3 cups shredded kale

2 cups shredded Brussels sprouts

½ cup Marcona almonds

⅓ cup shredded vegan Parmesan

1 batch **30-Second Red Wine Vinaigrette** (page 197)

1. To a small bowl, combine the red onion, apple cider vinegar, and ½ cup water. Set aside to allow the onions to pickle while you make the salad.

2. To a microwave-safe bowl, add the drained chickpeas, olive oil, smoked paprika, salt, and pepper. Microwave for about 1 minute or until warmed through.

3. To a large salad bowl, add the kale, Brussels sprouts, almonds, warmed chickpeas, and vegan Parmesan, if using. Remove the pickled red onions from the liquid and add to the salad bowl. Discard the liquid.

4. Toss the salad with the dressing, and enjoy.

> **Note**
>
> Store this salad in an airtight container in the fridge for up to 4 days.

the fiesta chop

SERVES 3

I freaking love a Mexican-inspired chopped salad, and this one is filled with all kinds of goodies. The hearty lentils, fresh and crunchy veggies, creamy avocado, sweet corn, and delicious dressing come together to make for a fiesta in your mouth.

prep time:
15 minutes

cook time:
2 minutes

1 cup corn

1 (15oz/425g) can brown or black lentils, drained and rinsed

1 large head romaine lettuce, chopped

1 cup diced tomato

1 large red bell pepper, ribs and seeds removed, diced

1 large green bell pepper, ribs and seeds removed, diced

1 large avocado, pit and skin removed, diced

⅓ cup chopped fresh cilantro

Juice of 1 lime

1 batch **Fiesta Dressing** (page 221)

⅓ cup shredded vegan Mexican-blend cheese, optional

1. In a small microwave-safe bowl, steam the corn by microwaving for 2 minutes. Let cool.

2. To a large salad bowl, add the lentils, lettuce, tomato, bell peppers, avocado, cilantro, and steamed corn. Squeeze the lime juice over the salad.

3. Top with the dressing and cheese, if using. Toss and enjoy!

warm

SALADS

perfectly cozy salads for cold weather

the zen bowl

SERVES 3

This salad truly warms the soul. The cooked vegetables and grains are grounding and nourishing and give an all-around Zen feeling. Black rice, otherwise known as "forbidden rice," has a nutty flavor, is a good source of iron and antioxidants, and contains more fiber than white rice! The combination of tender kale, roasted curried cauliflower, hearty black rice, and Balsamic Tahini Dressing will have you feeling good all day long. Feel free to add a protein like sautéed tofu, or serve this as a side salad with dinner.

prep time:
15 minutes

cook time:
30 minutes

1 cup black rice

1 large head cauliflower, cut into florets

1½ tbsp olive oil, divided

1 tsp salt, divided

½ tsp ground black pepper, divided

¼ tsp chili powder

¼ tsp curry powder

¼ tsp ground ginger

½ tsp paprika

½ tsp garlic powder

½ tsp ground turmeric

1 head curly kale, destemmed and chopped

1 batch **Balsamic Tahini Dressing** (page 245)

1. Cook the black rice according to package instructions. Fluff with a fork and set aside.

2. Preheat the oven to 425°F (220°C) and line a baking sheet with parchment paper.

3. On the lined baking sheet, spread out the cauliflower florets. Drizzle with 1 tablespoon of olive oil and sprinkle with ½ teaspoon of salt, ¼ teaspoon of pepper, chili powder, curry powder, ginger, paprika, garlic powder, and turmeric. Mix well and roast on the middle rack of the oven for 25 minutes, until golden brown and tender. Remove from the oven and set aside.

4. To a large pan over medium-high heat, add the remaining ½ tablespoon of olive oil, the remaining ½ teaspoon of salt, the remaining ¼ teaspoon of pepper, and the chopped kale. Sauté for about 4 minutes and remove from the heat.

5. In a large bowl, combine the sautéed kale, roasted cauliflower, and cooked black rice. Pour as little or as much of the Balsamic Tahini Dressing as you want over the top. Toss to combine, and enjoy!

rooting for you

SERVES 4–6

Root vegetables are an important but often overlooked aspect of one's diet. Root veggies are special—they're grown underground and packed with everything from iron, magnesium, and potassium to anti-inflammatory properties. The majority of root vegetables have a low-glycemic index, which is a fancy way of saying they'll help keep your blood sugar steady. This salad is grounding, warming, hearty, and amazing for digestive health.

prep time:
20 minutes

cook time:
30 minutes

1 medium sweet potato, peeled and diced

1 medium purple potato, diced

2 large carrots, diced

2 medium turnips, peeled and diced

1 tbsp maple syrup

2 tbsp olive oil

1 tsp garlic powder

2 tsp salt

¼ tsp ground black pepper

3 cups cooked farro

1 batch **Green Goodness Dressing** (page 242)

Pomegranate arils, optional

1. Preheat the oven to 450°F (230°C). Line a baking sheet with parchment paper.

2. To the lined baking sheet, evenly spread out the diced sweet and purple potatoes, carrots, and turnips. Add the maple syrup, olive oil, garlic powder, salt, and pepper. Mix well to ensure even coating. Roast in the oven for 30 minutes or until tender and golden.

3. In a large bowl, mix the hot roasted vegetables and cooked farro together. Drizzle on the Green Goodness Dressing, and sprinkle pomegranate arils over the top. Enjoy, bestie.

garlicky shrooms + greens

SERVES 3

If you need a side dish for your healthy dinner, this mushroom-based salad is going to be your new favorite. The earthy umami flavors will keep you coming back for more, not to mention the mushrooms are packed with vitamin D and help reduce breast cancer risk.

prep time:
10 minutes

cook time:
15 minutes

1 tbsp olive oil

3 cloves garlic, minced

2 shallots, diced

2 cups sliced baby bella mushrooms

2 cups sliced cremini mushrooms

1 cup sliced shiitake mushrooms

½ tsp salt

1 tsp chopped fresh thyme

Pinch of ground black pepper

3 cups baby spinach

1 tbsp balsamic vinegar

1 tbsp soy sauce

Toasted pine nuts, optional

Vegan Parmesan, optional

1. In a large nonstick pan over medium heat, add in the olive oil, garlic, and shallots. Sauté for a few minutes until the shallots are translucent and the garlic is aromatic.

2. Increase the heat a bit, then add the baby bella, cremini, and shiitake mushrooms. Sauté until the moisture in the mushrooms is released and they're golden brown. Season mushrooms with salt, thyme, and pepper.

3. When the mushrooms are done cooking, turn off the heat, then add the spinach and mix until spinach gently wilts.

4. Add the balsamic vinegar and soy sauce. Mix until combined well, then transfer to a bowl or salad platter.

5. Garnish with toasted pine nuts and vegan Parmesan if you'd like—it's also delicious as is. Enjoy warm.

roasted carrot salad
(with chimichurri)

SERVES 6

Warm, sweet, and savory roasted carrots are tender and delicious on top of hearty, earthy lentils. The fresh parsley chimichurri complements the dish perfectly. I like to make this for the holidays—it's always a hit and looks beautiful on a platter.

prep time:
20 minutes

cook time:
30 minutes

16oz (450g) large rainbow carrots, washed and peeled

1 tbsp date syrup

2 tbsp olive oil, divided

1 tsp salt, divided

⅛ tsp ground black pepper

½ tsp garlic powder

2 cups cooked black lentils (see note)

2 tbsp tahini

½ batch **Cha Cha Chimichurri** (page 222)

¼ cup pomegranate arils

3 tbsp pistachios, shelled and chopped

1. Preheat the oven to 425°F (220°C). Line a baking sheet with parchment paper.

2. Directly on the baking sheet, toss the carrots with the date syrup, 1 tablespoon of olive oil, ½ teaspoon of salt, pepper, and garlic powder. Spread the carrots evenly over the lined baking sheet. Roast for 30 minutes or until tender and well roasted.

3. In a medium bowl, mix the cooked lentils with the remaining 1 tablespoon of olive oil and the remaining ½ teaspoon of salt.

4. On a platter, spread the lentils evenly over the bottom. Add the hot roasted carrots on top, drizzle with the tahini, pour on the Cha Cha Chimichurri, and garnish with the pomegranate arils and pistachios. Enjoy!

> **Note**
>
> This recipe can be made with canned or freshly cooked lentils. If using canned lentils, make sure to drain the juices and rinse them first. If using fresh lentils, follow package instructions to cook them. I used two 15oz cans of black lentils.

cuban cutie

SERVES 4

Warm, flavorful, spicy, savory, and a little sweet, the Cuban Cutie salad bowl is going to be your new favorite dinner. It's packed with protein from the black beans, carbs from the rice and crispy warm plantains, and fiber from the veggies. This is a very well-balanced, satiating meal.

prep time:
15 minutes

cook time:
30 minutes

1 large red bell pepper, ribs and seeds removed, sliced

1 tsp cooking oil

¼ tsp chili powder

¼ tsp ground cumin

¼ tsp garlic powder

1 (14oz/397g) can black beans, drained and rinsed

1 large beefsteak tomato, diced

1 large white onion, finely diced

1 large avocado, pit and skin removed, sliced

1 batch **Avocado Cilantro Lime Dressing** (page 226)

Chopped fresh cilantro, optional

Juice of 1 lime, optional

For the cilantro-lime rice

1 cup brown or white rice

3 tbsp lime juice

⅓ cup finely chopped cilantro

½ tsp garlic powder

½ tsp salt

1 tbsp avocado oil or olive oil

For the plantains

3 tbsp olive oil

2 sweet plantains, sliced diagonally ½-in (1.25cm) thick

¼ tsp salt

1. **Make the cilantro-lime rice.** Cook the rice according to package instructions. 1 cup dry rice will yield 3 cups cooked.

2. Once the rice is cooked, add the remaining cilantro-rice ingredients and mix well to combine. Set aside.

3. **Cook the plantains.** To a large nonstick pan over medium heat, add the olive oil.

4. Once the oil is hot, add the plantain slices to the pan and cook for a few minutes on each side until deeply golden brown.

5. Line a plate with a paper towel and transfer the plantains to it. Sprinkle the salt over the top and set aside.

6. **Prepare the salad.** To a large nonstick pan, add the bell peppers, cooking oil, chili powder, ground cumin, and garlic powder. Sauté until the peppers are tender. Set aside.

7. Heat the black beans in a small pot on the stove or in a microwave-safe bowl in the microwave.

8. Assemble the bowls, layering with cilantro-lime rice, cooked plantains, warm black beans, tomato, onion, sautéed peppers, and avocado slices. Drizzle the Avocado Cilantro Lime Dressing over the top.

9. Garnish with cilantro and lime juice if desired. Enjoy, cutie!

pizza salad, please

SERVES 4

I am such a pizza girlie. There is nothing quite like a crispy slice of 'za. But as you know, I am also very much a salad girlie. This is a dinner I make all the time because it's super easy. I make a salad with my favorite pizza toppings, then I bake a crust and use it as a scoop to eat my pizza-topping salad. Genius, right?!

prep time:
20 minutes

cook time:
10 minutes

1 tsp olive oil

1 tsp minced fresh garlic

4 cups sliced mushrooms of your choice

2 cups arugula

2 cups chopped romaine lettuce

½ cup jarred roasted red peppers

½ cup sliced olives of your choice

½ cup diced tomato

½ cup sliced jarred banana peppers, chopped

1 batch **Tomato Parmesan Vinaigrette** (page 194)

Fresh basil, optional

Vegan Parmesan, optional

1 store-bought pizza crust, baked according to package instructions

1. In a large pan over medium-high heat, add the olive oil, garlic, and mushrooms. Sauté until the water cooks out of the mushrooms and they are golden, about 8 to 10 minutes. Set aside.

2. In a large salad bowl, combine the arugula, romaine lettuce, roasted red peppers, olives, diced tomato, banana peppers, and sautéed mushrooms. Toss with as much of the Tomato Parmesan Vinaigrette as you like.

3. Garnish with fresh basil and vegan Parmesan, if using.

4. Cut the pizza crust into pie triangles and use it as a vessel to dip into your salad.

sunrise breakfast salad

SERVES 2–4

Turning brunch into a salad is honestly genius. It combines all your favorite brunch classics into a savory, satiating, protein-packed breakfast that will keep you full for hours. This is perfect for slow mornings, like on weekends. My favorite part of this bowl is the everything-bagel croutons—YUM!

prep time:
10 minutes

cook time:
30 minutes

2 russet potatoes, cubed into 1-inch pieces

2 tbsp olive oil, divided, plus a drizzle for serving

1½ tsp salt, divided

1 tsp ground black pepper

1 tsp garlic powder, divided

½ tsp paprika

1 everything bagel, cut into bite-size pieces

Olive oil spray

½ cup diced yellow onion

1 block extra-firm tofu, crumbled

½ tsp ground turmeric

1 tbsp nutritional yeast

1 tsp smoked paprika

2 tbsp nondairy milk

1 cup arugula

2 cups spinach

Juice of ½ lemon

1 tomato, diced

1 avocado, pit and skin removed, sliced

Hot sauce, optional

1. Preheat the oven to 450°F (230°C) and line a baking sheet with parchment paper.

2. To one half of the baking sheet, add the cubed potatoes. Season with 1 tablespoon of olive oil, ½ teaspoon of salt, pepper, ½ teaspoon of garlic powder, and the paprika. Roast for 25 minutes until deeply brown and tender. About 10 minutes before they are done, add the everything bagel pieces to the other half of the sheet. Spray with olive oil spray and bake until golden and crispy. Then remove from the oven and set aside.

3. To a large nonstick pan over medium heat, add the remaining 1 tablespoon of olive oil and the diced onion, and sauté until the onion is translucent. Turn the heat up to high and add in the crumbled tofu, the remaining 1 teaspoon of salt, the remaining ½ teaspoon of garlic powder, as well as the turmeric, nutritional yeast, smoked paprika, and nondairy milk. Sauté for about 5 minutes. Remove the tofu scramble from the heat and set aside.

4. Split the greens up between serving bowls and drizzle a little olive oil and lemon juice over top. Add the diced tomato and sliced avocado.

5. Top with the tofu scramble and roasted potatoes, and garnish with everything-bagel croutons. Drizzle on a little hot sauce, if using, and enjoy!

warm salad-veggie muffins

SERVES 12

If you're not in the mood for a raw salad in a typical salad form or you want your veggies on the go, try making these delicious savory muffins. They're made with five different vegetables, flavorful herbs, and vegan cheese. If you're gluten-free, use gluten-free all-purpose flour instead of whole-wheat.

prep time:
25 minutes

cook time:
25 minutes

2 tbsp ground flaxseed

1½ cups whole-wheat flour

½ cup almond flour

1 tbsp baking powder

½ tsp baking soda

2 tsp salt

½ tsp ground black pepper

1 tsp dried oregano

1 tsp dried basil

1 tsp garlic powder

1 cup unsweetened soy milk

¼ cup olive oil

1 tbsp apple cider vinegar

1 cup finely chopped fresh spinach

½ cup grated carrot

½ cup diced bell pepper (red or yellow)

¼ cup chopped green onions

¼ cup chopped fresh parsley

¼ cup quartered cherry tomatoes

¼ cup grated vegan Parmesan

Balsamic and oil, or dairy-free butter, for serving

1. Preheat the oven to 375°F (190°C). Line a muffin tin with paper liners or lightly grease with oil.

2. In a small bowl, mix the ground flaxseed with 6 tablespoons of water, and let sit for 5 to 10 minutes until the flaxseed becomes gel-like.

3. In a large mixing bowl, whisk together the whole-wheat flour, almond flour, baking powder, baking soda, salt, black pepper, dried oregano, dried basil, and garlic powder. Add in the soy milk, olive oil, and apple cider vinegar. Mix again, making sure not to overmix.

4. Gently fold in the spinach, carrot, bell pepper, green onions, parsley, cherry tomatoes, and vegan Parmesan.

5. Evenly divide the batter among the muffin cups, filling each to about ¾ full. Top with shredded vegan Parmesan, if you desire. (I use the Violife brand.)

6. Bake for 20 to 25 minutes, until a toothpick inserted into the center of a muffin comes out clean.

7. Let the muffins cool for about 5 minutes before transferring to a wire rack to cool completely.

8. Enjoy your muffins warm with balsamic and oil or dairy-free butter. Store cooled muffins in an airtight container at room temperature for up to 3 days.

cashew grilled cheese sandwich
(with tomato salad)

SERVES 1

Okay, so I lied. This salad isn't warm—the part that is warm is the grilled cheese. Cut me some slack, though, because this combination is worth it. Warm grilled cheese paired with a gorgeous tomato salad is always a good decision. Make this a pesto grilled cheese by adding pesto to the sandwich like I did!

prep time:
15 minutes

cook time:
10 minutes

½ cup raw cashews

2 tbsp nutritional yeast

2 tsp lemon juice

½ tsp garlic powder

1 tsp salt

2 slices of sourdough bread

1 tbsp salted vegan butter

1 large heirloom tomato, cut into wedges

1 cup fresh basil leaves, cut in a chiffonade

1 tsp extra-virgin olive oil

1 tsp balsamic vinegar

Pinch of salt and ground black pepper

Pesto, for serving, optional

1. Bring a small pot of water to a boil (1 cup). Add in the cashews and boil for 5 minutes to soften them.

2. In a food processor, add the boiled cashews, nutritional yeast, lemon juice, garlic powder, salt, and 2 tablespoons water. Blend until smooth.

3. Spread the blended cashew mixture on one slice of sourdough, then top with the other slice. Spread vegan butter on the outer sides of the sandwich.

4. In a nonstick pan over medium heat, fry the sandwich until each side is golden brown, about 3 minutes per side.

5. In small bowl, combine the tomato wedges, basil, olive oil, balsamic vinegar, salt, and pepper. Mix well.

6. Enjoy your homemade plant-based grilled cheese and fresh tomato salad!

seasonal

SALADS

a salad for every time of year

veggie-burger salad

SERVES 3

Turn your burgers into a Veggie-Burger Salad with this recipe. This salad is basically a deconstructed burger with everyone's favorite burger toppings, from onions to pickles to animal-style sauce. Everyone prefers a different kind of burger, so choose your favorite to pair with this meal!

prep time:
15 minutes

cook time:
30 minutes

1 sweet potato, cut into fries

1 purple or regular potato, cut into fries

2 tbsp olive oil

½ tsp salt

¼ tsp ground black pepper

3 veggie burgers (your favorite kind)

1–2 avocados, pit and skin removed, sliced

½ cup sliced red onion or chopped white onion

3 dill pickles, sliced

1 cup diced tomato

3 cups lettuce of choice (romaine, shredded iceberg, green leaf, mixed greens)

For the animal-style sauce

½ cup ketchup

¼ cup vegan mayonnaise or plain vegan yogurt

1 tbsp yellow mustard

1. Preheat the oven to 425°F (220°C). Line a baking sheet with parchment paper.

2. On the lined baking sheet, spread out the sweet and purple potato fries, and coat evenly with olive oil, salt, and pepper. Bake for 25 minutes until the potatoes are tender, golden, and crispy. Remove from the oven.

3. While the fries are baking, cook the veggie burgers according to package instructions.

4. Assemble your burger bowls with a cooked veggie burger and top with avocado, onion, pickles, tomatoes, lettuce, and roasted fries.

5. **Mix the animal-style sauce** ingredients together in a small bowl and drizzle on top of the salad bowls. Enjoy!

> **Note**
> Fry-cut veggies should measure about ¼ x ¼ x 2½ inches (6 mm x 6 mm x 6.25 cm).

the peachy

SERVES 4

Nothing screams summer like this gorgeous, glistening, juicy salad. This is an absolutely perfect appetizer to serve guests because it's easy to make yet very impressive. I like to serve this as shown, since the peaches and avocado are delicate. The dish is pulled together with a drizzle of balsamic glaze and olive oil . . . yes, please.

prep time:
5 minutes

cook time:
5 minutes

2 medium peaches, sliced into wedges

2 large avocados, pit and skin removed, sliced

1 large heirloom tomato, sliced in wedges

½ cup fresh basil leaves

2 tbsp balsamic glaze

2 tbsp extra-virgin olive oil

Pinch of flaky salt

Pinch of freshly ground black pepper

1. On a hot indoor or outdoor grill or stove, char the peach wedges for 1 to 2 minutes per side until they have grill marks or they turn golden.

2. Plate your salad! Create a beautiful platter by nestling together peach wedges, avocado slices, tomato wedges, and basil. Repeat until you've used all the ingredients. Use a large platter if you're serving many guests.

3. Drizzle the balsamic glaze and olive oil over top, then season with flaky salt and black pepper. Enjoy immediately!

don't be crabby

SERVES 6

Nothing screams summer like some crab cakes and slaw. This slaw has the perfect combination of sweet pineapple, crunchy cabbage, and crisp bell pepper. It's topped off with a plant-based crab cake made from hearts of palm for the freshest summer salad that's perfect for summer backyard dinners. I like to pair this with freshly grilled corn on the cob.

prep time:
20 minutes

1 cup finely chopped purple cabbage

1 cup finely chopped green cabbage

1 red bell pepper, ribs and seeds removed, finely diced

1 yellow bell pepper, ribs and seeds removed, finely diced

2 avocados, pit and skin removed, diced

½ cup chopped fresh cilantro

¼ cup sliced green onion

1 batch hearts of palm crab cakes (*HealthyGirl Kitchen* cookbook, page 216)

Juice of 1 lemon

For the dressing

2 tbsp extra-virgin olive oil or avocado oil

2 tbsp vegan mayonnaise or plain vegan yogurt

3 tbsp lemon juice

1 tsp Dijon mustard

2 tsp salt

¼ tsp pepper

1. **Make the dressing.** To a large salad bowl, add the dressing ingredients and whisk until well combined.

2. **Prepare the slaw.** To the bowl with the dressing, add the cabbage, bell peppers, avocados, cilantro, and green onion, and toss.

3. Serve the slaw with the crab cakes on top and drizzle with fresh lemon juice. Enjoy!

layered mexican salad

SERVES 8–10

Now *this* is a party salad. This Layered Mexican Salad is great if you're hosting and need a fun addition to a meal. Make this for anything from Cinco de Mayo, to a family holiday, a fun gathering, or just a BBQ with friends.

prep time:
40 minutes

cook time:
5 minutes

3 cups cooked black or brown lentils

¼ cup salsa

1 tbsp chili powder

1 tsp ground cumin

1 tsp smoked paprika

1¼ tsp garlic powder, divided

2 tsp salt, divided

¼ tsp ground black pepper

2 cups cooked white or brown rice

1 head romaine lettuce, shredded

½ white onion, diced

2 large beefsteak tomatoes, diced

¼ cup chopped fresh cilantro

2 tbsp lime juice

1 large orange bell pepper, ribs and seeds removed, diced

2 cups steamed or grilled corn kernels

2 large avocados, pit and skin removed, diced

1 cup sliced black olives

½ cup shredded vegan Mexican-blend cheese, optional

1 batch **Avocado Cilantro Lime Dressing** (page 226)

1. In a large pan over medium-high heat, add the cooked lentils, salsa, chili powder, cumin, smoked paprika, 1 teaspoon garlic powder, 1 teaspoon salt, and pepper. Sauté for about 5 minutes. Remove the "taco-meat" lentils from the heat and set aside.

2. In a large glass serving bowl (like for trifles) or a 9 x 13-inch (23 x 23 cm) glass baking dish, begin layering the salad. Add the cooked rice to the bottom and spread evenly.

3. Next, evenly add the taco-meat lentils over the rice and layer the shredded romaine next.

4. In a separate small bowl, make pico de gallo by combining the diced onion, diced tomatoes, cilantro, lime juice, remaining ¼ teaspoon garlic powder, and remaining 1 teaspoon salt. Mix well. Layer the pico de gallo over the top of the romaine lettuce.

5. Next, add the bell pepper, the corn kernels, and the diced avocados, layering each evenly.

6. Last but not least, sprinkle the black olives and vegan cheese over the top.

7. Serve with a side of the Avocado Cilantro Lime Dressing. Enjoy, party people!

the fall edit

SERVES 4–5

Nothing screams fall like pumpkin. This sweet, savory, and cozy salad is perfect on a crisp fall day. If you're feeling "scrappy"—shout-out to my bestie Carleigh from PlantYou—you can roast fresh pumpkin seeds as a topping. Don't have a pumpkin on hand? Sub in a large sweet potato instead.

prep time:
30 minutes

cook time:
40 minutes

1 sugar pumpkin or sweet potato, cubed

3 medium fresh beets, peeled and cubed

2 tbsp olive oil

1 tsp salt

⅛ tsp ground black pepper

1 tsp garlic powder

¼ tsp ground cinnamon

1 tbsp maple syrup

3 cups spinach

1 batch **Taylor's Lemon Rosemary Vinaigrette** (page 202) or **Balsamic Baby** dressing (page 225)

⅓ cup crumbled vegan feta

¼ cup roasted, salted pumpkin seeds

1. Preheat the oven to 450°F (230°C). Line a large baking sheet with parchment paper.

2. In a large bowl, toss the cubed pumpkin and beets with olive oil, salt, pepper, garlic powder, cinnamon, and maple syrup. To the lined baking sheet, spread the pumpkin and beets evenly. Roast for 35 to 40 minutes, until fork-tender. Remove from the oven and set aside.

3. In another large bowl, add the spinach and half the dressing. Toss to combine.

4. On a serving platter, place the dressed spinach. Top with the roasted pumpkin and beets, vegan feta, and pumpkin seeds.

5. Drizzle the remaining half of the dressing over top of the salad, and enjoy!

delicata squash salad

SERVES 4–6

This is one for the holiday season. It's festive and beautiful, it impresses a crowd, and it has simple, tasteful ingredients. This elevated salad is gorgeous when arranged on a large platter. You can bring this to any holiday party you're invited to!

prep time:
10 minutes

cook time:
25 minutes

1 delicata squash or acorn squash, cut into ½-inch thick half moons or wedges

1 tbsp olive oil

1 tsp salt

1 tsp garlic powder

⅛ tsp ground black pepper

1 head radicchio

1 cup cooked pearled couscous

½ cup golden raisins

3 tbsp chopped walnuts

1 batch **Balsamic Baby** dressing (page 225)

1. Preheat the oven to 400°F (200°C). Line a baking sheet with parchment paper.

2. On the lined baking sheet, arrange the squash, and toss with olive oil, salt, garlic powder, and pepper. Bake for 25 minutes, until the squash is golden and fork-tender. Remove from the oven and set aside.

3. Gently separate the radicchio leaves from the head and arrange them on a large platter.

4. Top the radicchio leaves with cooked couscous, the roasted squash, raisins, and chopped walnuts.

5. Pour the Balsamic Baby dressing on top, and enjoy!

wintergirl salad

SERVES 2

This salad is the perfect mix of crunchy and sweet produce that is available come winter. The shredded Brussels sprouts are a great way to sneak in some gut-healthy cruciferous vegetables. The crisp, sweet pear works perfectly with the savory red onion and crunchy Brussels sprouts.

prep time:
10 minutes

2 cups mixed greens

1 cup thinly shredded Brussels sprouts

1 medium pear, thinly sliced

2 tbsp dried blueberries

¼ cup thinly sliced red onion

1 batch **30-Second Red Wine Vinaigrette** (page 197)

1. To a large bowl, add all of the salad ingredients.

2. Drizzle on as much or as little of the 30-Second Red Wine Vinaigrette as you'd like, and toss to combine.

3. Enjoy fresh!

> **Note**
> For the mixed greens, spring mix is a good option.

malibu salad

SERVES 2

One of my best friends, Jolie, and her family own an award-winning Jewish deli called The Stage. I grew up eating there, and during our high school lunch breaks, we'd always drive over to squeeze in a delicious lunch. My go-to order was the Malibu Salad, and we'd share a side of shoestring fries. I asked Jolie if I could include the Malibu Salad in this book, because it is in fact life-changing, and she said she'd be honored. So, Jo, this one's for you!

prep time:
10 minutes

5 cups mixed baby greens

1 Granny Smith apple, sliced

1 avocado, pit and skin removed, sliced

2 tbsp slivered almonds

¼ cup sun-dried cherries

⅓ cup crumbled vegan feta

1 batch **Perfect Poppy Seed Dressing** (page 217)

1. To a large bowl, add the mixed greens. Add the apples and avocado over the greens, then sprinkle on the almonds, dried cherries, and crumbled vegan feta.

2. Drizzle on as much or as little of the Perfect Poppy Seed Dressing as you'd like, and enjoy the Malibu, boo.

spring niçoise salad

SERVES 4

A traditional Niçoise salad has hard-boiled eggs and tuna, but I was determined to make a plant-based version that's just as good. Make this for a girls' lunch, a holiday brunch, or simply to enjoy at home on a pretty spring day. Light, fresh, and crisp, this is sure to be a favorite.

prep time:
10 minutes

cook time:
20 minutes

8oz French green beans, trimmed

1 cup halved baby potatoes

3 cups chopped red leaf lettuce

1 cup cherry tomatoes, halved

1 cup thinly sliced radishes

1 cup marinated artichoke hearts, drained

1 (15oz/425g) can chickpeas, drained and rinsed

½ cup thinly sliced red onion

½ cup mixed Greek olives, pitted

1 avocado, pit and skin removed, sliced

1 cup sliced cucumber

3 tbsp capers

Fresh chives, optional

Fresh dill, optional

1 batch **30-Second Red Wine Vinaigrette** (page 197)

1. Bring a medium pot of salted water to a boil over high heat, then add the green beans. Cook for 3 to 4 minutes, until just tender but still crisp. With tongs, transfer the green beans to a bowl of ice water. Once cold, drain the beans.

2. To the still boiling pot of salted water, add the baby potatoes and boil for 10 to 15 minutes, until fork-tender. Drain the potatoes and set aside.

3. Assemble the salad by arranging the red leaf lettuce on a platter. In sections, artfully arrange the drained green beans, cooked potatoes, tomatoes, radishes, artichoke hearts, chickpeas, red onion, olives, avocado, cucumber, and capers.

4. Garnish with fresh chives and dill, if using. Drizzle the dressing over top and enjoy fresh.

no-lettuce

SALADS

never have a soggy salad again

broccoli caesar salad

SERVES 2

This is going to be your new favorite way to eat broccoli. Instead of using lettuce as the base of the Caesar salad, I opt for broccoli in this recipe. I like to roast the broccoli to make it nice and crispy. Also, roasted chickpeas make the best healthy "croutons"! Once you make this Caesar salad with broccoli, you won't be able to stop making it.

prep time:
15 minutes

cook time:
30 minutes

1 head broccoli, cut into 1-inch florets

1 (15oz/425g) can chickpeas, drained and rinsed

Olive oil spray

½ tsp salt

⅛ tsp ground black pepper

1 tsp garlic powder

1 batch **Hemp Seed Caesar Dressing** (page 213)

Vegan Parmesan, grated or shredded

1. Preheat the oven to 425°F (220°C). Line a baking sheet with parchment paper.

2. To the lined baking sheet, add the broccoli and chickpeas. Coat with olive oil spray and season with salt, pepper, and garlic powder. Roast for 25 to 30 minutes, until broccoli is tender and golden. Remove from the oven.

3. In a large bowl, combine the roasted broccoli and chickpeas with as much or as little of the dressing as you'd like. Garnish with vegan Parmesan, and enjoy!

date-me salad

SERVES 4

If you want to impress someone, this salad will make them want to date you—it's *that* good. We love kale-based salads around here, and you want to know why? You guessed it! Because it won't get soggy in the fridge. Everything from the crisp veggies and sweet, chewy dates to the creamy avocado, vegan feta cheese, and irresistible dressing makes this salad addictive.

prep time:
15 minutes

½ red onion, thinly sliced

3 tbsp apple cider vinegar

1 head kale, shredded

1 tbsp extra-virgin olive oil

1 (15oz/425g) can chickpeas, drained and rinsed

⅓ cup chopped dates

1 cup chopped cucumber

1 ripe avocado, pit and skin removed, cubed

¼ cup chopped walnuts

½ cup crumbled vegan feta

For the dressing

¼ cup extra-virgin olive oil

2 tbsp red wine vinegar

1 tbsp tahini

2 tsp Dijon mustard

2 tsp maple syrup

¼ tsp salt

Freshly ground black pepper

1. To a small bowl, add the onion and apple cider vinegar. Add 1 tablespoon of water at a time until the onions are covered. Set aside.

2. To a large salad bowl, add the shredded kale and olive oil. Massage the kale with your hands to make it more tender for 1 to 2 minutes.

3. Add the chickpeas, dates, cucumber, avocado, walnuts, and feta to the salad bowl. Drain the onions, then top the salad with the pickled onions.

4. **Make the dressing.** In a small bowl or jar, combine the dressing ingredients. Whisk or shake to combine, and pour over the top of the assembled salad! Enjoy!

> **Note**
> Keep in the fridge in an airtight container for up to 3 days.

gut-health slaw

SERVES 4

Getting enough vegetables, especially cruciferous veggies, is hard for a lot of us. The secret is to shred all of your veggies super thin. The cabbage, fresh fennel, beets, carrots, and parsley in this recipe help to maintain the good bacteria in your gut microbiome and reduce inflammation. This crispy, crunchy, fresh slaw tastes even better the next day, after it's marinated overnight in the fridge.

prep time:
20 minutes

chill time:
4 hours to overnight

1 batch **Gut-Healthy Vinaigrette** (page 205)

2 cups shredded purple cabbage

2 cups shredded green cabbage

1 cup thinly sliced fresh fennel bulb

1 cup thinly sliced or shredded fresh beets

1 cup shredded carrots

½ cup chopped parsley

1. Make the dressing in the bottom of a bowl or large container. Add the cabbage, fennel, beets, carrots, and parsley.

2. Toss and combine well.

3. Cover the container or bowl and let the slaw marinate for at least 4 hours or overnight if you want it extra yummy!

4. Keeps for 4 days in an airtight container in the fridge.

Note

Use a mandoline on the thinnest setting to easily slice or shred the purple cabbage, green cabbage, fennel bulb, carrot, and beet.

---

cowgirl caviar

SERVES 8–12

Here's what you're going to do: get a group of girlfriends together, make a batch of this Cowgirl Caviar, get out a big-ass bowl of tortilla chips, make some mocktails or frozen margaritas, and enjoy. This doesn't take long to make and is always a hit.

prep time:
20 minutes

cook time:
2 minutes

1½ cups corn kernels, steamed or grilled (see note)

1 large red bell pepper, ribs and seeds removed, diced

1 large yellow bell pepper, ribs and seeds removed, diced

1 large orange bell pepper, ribs and seeds removed, diced

1 (14oz/397g) can black beans, drained and rinsed

1 (14oz/397g) can black-eyed peas, drained and rinsed

½ cup chopped fresh cilantro

½ red onion, finely diced

3 tbsp lime juice

1 tsp cumin

½ tsp garlic powder

1 tsp salt

Pinch of ground black pepper

1. To a large salad bowl, add all the ingredients and toss well to combine.

2. Enjoy! Store in the fridge for up to 4 days in an airtight container.

Note

To steam the corn, you can cut the corn kernels off the cob, place in a microwave-safe bowl, and microwave for about 2 minutes. There are other ways to steam corn, but this is the quickest. Alternatively, you can grill the corn and then cut it off the cob.

edamame crunch salad

SERVES 2

Crunchy, crisp, fresh, and filled with good-for-you plant protein, this Edamame Crunch Salad is the perfect quick main course for lunch. This is delicious paired with grilled tofu but also stands perfectly on its own.

prep time:
10 minutes

cook time:
5 minutes

½ cup quinoa

2 cups edamame, steamed and de-shelled

1 cup snap peas, sliced thin

1 cup diced red bell pepper

1 cup diced cucumber

½ cup salted roasted cashews

¼ cup chopped fresh cilantro

2 tbsp furikake

2 tbsp rice vinegar

2 tsp toasted sesame oil

1 tsp agave syrup

1 tbsp soy sauce

Salt, to taste

1. In a large skillet over medium-high heat, add the quinoa and toast it, stirring and tossing every few seconds until it is golden brown or starts popping, which takes about 5 minutes. Remove from the heat.

2. To a salad bowl, add the edamame, snap peas, bell pepper, cucumber, cashews, cilantro, and toasted quinoa.

3. In a small bowl, whisk together the furikake, rice vinegar, sesame oil, agave syrup, and soy sauce. Drizzle the dressing over the salad.

4. Add salt to taste.

5. Toss and enjoy.

> **Note**
> Refrigerate for up to 4 days
> in an airtight container.

dill pickle potato salad

SERVES 4-6

If you need a springy salad to bring to a potluck, a barbecue, or a lake or beach day, *this* is the salad to make. Everyone likes potato salad—it's familiar, it's classic, and it's beyond delicious. The secret to this potato salad is using a little bit of vegan yogurt instead of mayonnaise. It has a very light dressing, so it's not as heavy as traditional potato salad. The best part is the crunchy dill pickles!

prep time:
20 minutes

cook time:
15 minutes

2lbs (907g) baby Yukon Gold potatoes

⅓ cup extra-virgin olive oil

2 tbsp white wine vinegar

¼ cup plain vegan yogurt

2 tbsp pickle brine

1 tbsp whole-grain Dijon mustard

½ red onion, thinly sliced into half circles

2 large dill pickles, diced

2 tbsp chopped fresh dill

¼ cup chopped fresh chives

Salt and freshly ground black pepper, to taste

1. Bring a medium pot of water to a boil over high heat. Salt the water generously.

2. Once the water is boiling, add the potatoes, reduce the heat to medium, and let cook until fork-tender, about 10 minutes. Drain the water and allow the potatoes to cool completely. If the potatoes were boiled whole, cut them in half. Set aside.

3. To a small bowl or jar, combine the olive oil, white wine vinegar, yogurt, pickle brine, and Dijon mustard. Whisk the dressing in a small bowl or shake in a jar. Set aside.

4. To a large serving bowl, add the potatoes, sliced red onions, diced pickles, dill, and chives.

5. Pour over as much or as little of the dressing as you'd like. Season with salt and pepper to taste.

6. Eat fresh or let it chill overnight in an airtight container in the fridge—it's even better the next day!

> **Note**
> The potatoes I use are tiny—about 1 inch (2.5cm) from top to bottom. I boil them whole, but if your baby potatoes are bigger, you'll want to cut them into quarters or halves before boiling.

greek potato salad

SERVES 4

I am dead serious when I say I could eat this dish every day. It combines buttery, hearty potatoes with Greek flavors like kalamata olives, fresh parsley, red onion, and a creamy Dairy-Free Tzatziki that is seriously drinkable. It's that good. This is a modern take on a traditional American potato salad, and I bet you'll never go back.

prep time:
15 minutes

cook time:
30 minutes

5 cups Yukon Gold potatoes, cut into 1-inch pieces

1 tbsp olive oil

Salt and ground black pepper, to taste

1 batch **Dairy-Free Tzatziki** (page 210)

½ cup sliced red onion

⅓ cup chopped sun-dried tomatoes

⅓ cup crumbled vegan feta

2 tbsp chopped flat-leaf parsley

1 tbsp capers

¼ cup chopped kalamata olives

1. Preheat the oven to 425°F (220°C). Line a baking sheet with parchment paper.

2. To the lined baking sheet, add the potatoes and spread evenly. Drizzle with olive oil, salt, and pepper. Mix to combine. Roast in the oven for 30 minutes or until crispy and golden brown. Set aside and let cool.

3. To a large bowl, add the roasted potatoes, then add as little or as much Dairy-Free Tzatziki as you'd like.

4. Add in the remaining ingredients. Mix gently, and enjoy!

cauli-power salad

SERVES 3

If you haven't used tender and delicious roasted cauliflower as the base of one of your salads before, it's about time. It is high in fiber—which is great for gut health—holds up well in the fridge, and is also nice for warmer weather. The Mediterranean-inspired flavors in this recipe make this salad a winner. This is a great side dish for a Shabbat dinner, a brunch, or an elevated dinner party.

prep time:
10 minutes

cook time:
30 minutes

1 head cauliflower, cut into 1-inch florets

5 tbsp olive oil, divided

1 tsp salt

½ tsp ground turmeric

¼ tsp ground cumin

1 tsp paprika

¼ tsp garlic powder

3 tbsp toasted pine nuts

4 dates, pitted and chopped

¼ cup diced red onion

1 tbsp chopped fresh mint

2 tbsp chopped fresh parsley

Juice of 1 lemon

Salt and ground black pepper, to taste

1. Preheat the oven to 425°F (220°C) and line a baking sheet with parchment paper.

2. To a large bowl, add the cauliflower florets, 2 tablespoons olive oil, salt, turmeric, cumin, paprika, and garlic powder. Toss to combine.

3. On the lined baking sheet, evenly spread out the seasoned cauliflower florets. Bake for 25 minutes or until the cauliflower is fork-tender. Remove from the oven and set aside.

4. To a small pan over medium heat, add the pine nuts and toast them for 3 to 5 minutes or until golden brown.

5. In a large bowl, combine the cauliflower, toasted pine nuts, dates, red onion, mint, and parsley, then transfer to a serving platter.

6. Drizzle the remaining 3 tablespoons of olive oil and the lemon juice over the top, then add additional salt and pepper to taste.

7. Store in the fridge in an airtight container for up to 4 days. Yum!

busygirl meal prep salad

SERVES 4

This recipe makes four lunches for the week. I call this a "set it and forget it" type of lunch. It's super helpful during your busiest days to have a nutrient-dense lunch prepped in the fridge and ready to go.

prep time:
5 minutes

cook time:
20 minutes

1 cup quinoa

2 large sweet potatoes, peeled and cubed

1 block high-protein extra-firm tofu, cubed

2 tbsp olive oil

1 tsp salt

1 tsp ground black pepper

1 tsp garlic powder

4 cups shredded kale

2 cups shredded carrots

1 batch **30-Second Red Wine Vinaigrette** (page 197)

1. Cook the quinoa according to package instructions and set aside. (See note.)

2. Preheat the oven to 400°F (200°C) and line a baking sheet with parchment paper.

3. To the lined baking sheet, add the sweet potatoes and tofu. Drizzle with the olive oil and season with the salt, pepper, and garlic powder. Bake for 20 minutes or until the sweet potato is fork-tender and golden. Remove from the oven and set aside.

4. To a large bowl, add the kale, carrots, and vinaigrette, and toss to combine to make a slaw.

5. Into four airtight containers, evenly portion the roasted tofu and potatoes, slaw, and quinoa.

6. Enjoy all week long! Happy prepping!

> **Note**
> For quinoa, 1 cup uncooked makes 4 cups cooked. You'll want about 1 cup of cooked quinoa in each container.

DRESSINGS

dress to impress with perfect pairings for every salad

tomato parmesan vinaigrette

YIELD: MAKES ABOUT 2 CUPS

This is the perfect earthy, savory dressing that can be used for anything from chopped salads to pasta salads. It is light, has a beautiful tomato flavor, and is a great way to use up tomatoes that are about to go bad.

Use for **Pizza Salad, Please**

¼ cup extra-virgin olive oil

2 tbsp red wine vinegar

1 large ripe beefsteak tomato

3 tbsp sun-dried tomatoes in olive oil

1 roughly chopped shallot, peeled and root-end removed

1 tsp Dijon mustard

1 tsp maple syrup

1 clove garlic

2 tbsp nutritional yeast

1 tsp salt

1 tsp minced fresh oregano, or ½ tsp dried oregano

¼ tsp ground black pepper

1. To a blender or food processor, add all the ingredients and blend until smooth.

> **Note**
> Store in an airtight container in the fridge for 2 to 3 days.

red wine vinegar

beefsteak tomato

black pepper

extra-virgin olive oil

salt

nutritional yeast

sun-dried tomatoes

shallot

maple syrup

garlic

Dijon mustard

oregano

extra-virgin olive oil

garlic powder

Dijon mustard

black pepper

salt

red wine vinegar

30-second red wine vinaigrette

YIELD: MAKES ABOUT ½ CUP

Everyone should know how to whip up a red wine vinaigrette, because it goes with just about everything and the ingredients are easy to keep in the pantry. In just 30 seconds, you'll have a delicious dressing that tastes like it's from a restaurant! Put this on anything from a classic salad to a pasta salad. You can even use it as a marinade for grilled tofu.

Use for **BusyGirl Brussels Salad, BusyGirl Meal Prep, Health-Nut Salad, Pizza Night Salad, Spring Niçoise Salad, Vegan Cobb Salad, Wild Rice Salad, WinterGirl Salad**

prep time:
1 minute

¼ cup extra-virgin olive oil

3 tbsp red wine vinegar

1 tsp Dijon mustard

¼ tsp garlic powder

Salt and ground black pepper, to taste

1. To a jar, bowl, or blender, add all the ingredients. Shake, whisk, or blend to combine. Yum!

> **Note**
> Store in the fridge in an airtight container or a jar for up to a month!

raspberry vinaigrette

YIELD: MAKES ABOUT 1 CUP

Adding raspberries to salad dressings not only results in a stunning salad, but it also adds about 7 grams of fiber and disease-fighting antioxidants to the dish. Raspberries provide natural sweetness without any added sugar, and this vinaigrette pairs beautifully with quinoa salads, leafy greens, orzo salads, and more.

Use for **Healthy Goddess Orzo, Superfood Brain-Booster Salad**

prep time:
5 minutes

1 cup raspberries

¼ cup extra-virgin olive oil

2 tbsp apple cider vinegar

1 tsp Dijon mustard

1 tbsp chopped shallot

Salt and ground black pepper, to taste

1. To a blender, add all the ingredients and blend until smooth. Enjoy!

Note

Store in an airtight container in the fridge for up to 4 days.

raspberries

extra-virgin olive oil

Dijon mustard

black pepper

salt

shallot

apple cider vinegar

agave syrup

sesame seeds

garlic

ginger

sesame oil

rice vinegar

avocado oil

soy sauce

sesame vinaigrette

YIELD: MAKES ABOUT ¾ CUP

This dressing is simple, light, and fresh, packed with delicious Asian-inspired flavors without the heaviness of a thick peanut dressing.

Use for **Chinese No-Chicken Salad**

prep time:
5 minutes

3 tbsp avocado oil

1 tbsp toasted sesame oil

3 tbsp rice vinegar

2 cloves garlic, minced

1 (2-in/5-cm) nub of fresh ginger root, grated

1 tbsp soy sauce

1 tbsp agave syrup or maple syrup

2 tbsp sesame seeds

1. In a small bowl, whisk together all the ingredients.

> **Note**
> Honey works in place of agave or maple syrup if you're not strictly vegan. Store leftover dressing in the refrigerator for up to 2 weeks in an airtight container.

taylor's lemon rosemary vinaigrette

YIELD: MAKES ABOUT ½ CUP

Taylor has been a part of the HealthyGirl team since 2021, and she has become one of my best friends. Not only do we look like sisters, but we're both major foodies. Our favorite part of recipe testing is eating all the food along the way. She is a literal recipe-developing genius and is always coming up with recipes, from sweet potato ice cream to tofu brownies. I told her I simply had to feature her Lemon Rosemary Dressing—it's delish.

Use for **The Fall Edit**

prep time:
5 minutes

¼ cup extra-virgin olive oil

1 tbsp white wine vinegar

2 tbsp lemon juice

½ tbsp date syrup or maple syrup

1 clove garlic, grated

1 tsp chopped fresh rosemary

1 tsp chopped fresh oregano

1 tbsp chopped fresh dill or 1 tsp dried dill

1 tsp chopped fresh thyme

1 tsp salt

Pinch of ground black pepper

1. To a bowl or jar, add all the ingredients, then whisk or shake to combine. Enjoy!

> **Note**
> Store in the fridge for up to 1 week in an airtight container or a jar.

lemon juice

date syrup

black pepper

extra-virgin olive oil

thyme

salt

garlic

oregano

dill

white wine vinegar

rosemary

extra-virgin olive oil

black pepper

garlic powder

salt

Dijon mustard

lemon juice

apple cider vinegar

maple syrup

gut-healthy vinaigrette

YIELD: MAKES ABOUT ⅔ CUP

Apple cider vinegar is one of those vinegars that can do wonders for our gut health, since it helps increase the hydrochloric acid in the stomach for improved digestion. This Gut-Healthy Vinaigrette wouldn't be complete without it! This is a very versatile dressing that is going to be a staple in your salad-making journey.

Use for **Gut-Health Slaw**

prep time:
5 minutes

¼ cup extra-virgin olive oil

2 tbsp apple cider vinegar

1 tbsp lemon juice

1 tsp Dijon mustard

1 tbsp maple syrup

1 tsp salt

¼ tsp ground black pepper

¼ tsp garlic powder

1. Add all the dressing ingredients to a bowl, blender, or jar. Whisk, blend, or shake to combine.

> **Note**
> I recommend using apple cider vinegar that's labeled as "with the mother." Store leftover dressing in the fridge for up to 2 weeks in an airtight container or a jar.

mediterranean mama dressing

YIELD: MAKES ABOUT ½ CUP

I made this dressing for one of my best friends, and she told me it was one of the best dressings she has ever had. It really is the best combination of sweet, herby, tangy, and rich flavors. Pair this with a classic fattoush salad or add to a pasta or orzo salad.

Use for Chopped Salad Pita, Fattoush Salad, Health-Nut Salad

prep time:
5 minutes

⅓ cup extra-virgin olive oil

3 tbsp lemon juice

1½ tsp pomegranate molasses (sub date syrup)

1½ tsp ground sumac

1 tsp dried mint flakes

¼ tsp garlic powder

Salt and ground black pepper, to taste

1. To a bowl or jar, add all the ingredients. Whisk or shake well to combine.

> **Note**
> Store in the fridge for up to 2 weeks in an airtight container or a jar.

black pepper

extra-virgin olive oil

salt

mint flakes

lemon juice

garlic powder

sumac

pomegranate
molasses

lemon juice

beet

salt

garlic

tahini

black pepper

Dijon mustard

avocado oil

anti-inflammatory beet dressing

YIELD: MAKES ABOUT 2 CUPS

Beets contain powerful antioxidants that are amazing at nourishing your body. Not only are they great for your health, but they also lend to a gorgeous-colored salad dressing. Sneak in some extra root veggies and make this ASAP.

Use for **Glow Bowl**

prep time:
10 minutes

⅓ cup avocado oil

1 medium fresh beet,
    peeled and chopped

1 tbsp tahini

1 clove garlic

3 tbsp lemon juice

2 tbsp water

1 tsp Dijon mustard

1 tsp salt

Pinch of ground black pepper

1. To a blender, add all the ingredients and blend until smooth.

> **Note**
> Store in the fridge for up to 5 days in an airtight container. Enjoy!

dairy-free tzatziki

YIELD: MAKES ABOUT 1 CUP

Creamy, dreamy, dairy-free tzatziki made with plant-based yogurt is one of my favorite go-tos! This is fresh, vibrant, and delicious to use with anything from veggies, to Greek pita sandwiches, to potato salad. Cucumber brightens this up and adds a much needed freshness. I used to love traditional tzatziki, especially at Greek restaurants, but this plant-based one is a real winner!

Use for Greek Potato Salad

prep time:
10 minutes

3 tbsp grated cucumber

½ cup plain vegan yogurt

2 tbsp vegan mayonnaise

1 tbsp extra-virgin olive oil

1 tsp lemon juice

2 cloves garlic, minced or microplaned

¼ tsp ground black pepper

1 tsp salt

2 tbsp finely chopped fresh dill

1. Place the grated cucumber in a paper towel or clean dish towel and squeeze out as much liquid as possible. Set aside the cucumber, and discard the liquid.

2. To a small bowl, add the yogurt, mayo, olive oil, lemon juice, garlic, pepper, and salt. Whisk until combined, then add in the cucumber and dill and mix again.

> **Note**
> Store in the fridge in an airtight container and enjoy for up to 3 days—but it's best enjoyed fresh!

yogurt

salt

cucumber

lemon juice

pepper

extra-virgin olive oil

garlic

mayonnaise

dill

capers + brine

lemon juice

Dijon mustard

garlic

salt

extra-virgin
olive oil

hemp seeds

black pepper

hemp seed caesar dressing

YIELD: MAKES ABOUT 2 CUPS

If you want one of the best vegan Caesar dressing recipes, this is it. It's creamy and perfectly salty, and it goes beautifully with a variety of salads and bowls. It can even be a dip for veggies. The best part: this is a nut-free version of my go-to Caesar dressing, so if you have a nut allergy, I got you.

Use for Broccoli Caesar Salad, Caesar Pasta Salad, Wedgie Veggie Salad

prep time:
5 minutes

1 cup hemp seeds

1 tbsp extra-virgin olive oil

2 tbsp lemon juice

2 or 3 cloves garlic

1 tbsp capers

1 tbsp caper brine

2 tsp Dijon mustard

½ tsp salt

¾ cup water

Freshly ground black pepper, to taste

1. To a high-speed blender, like a Vitamix, add all the ingredients and blend on high until completely smooth and creamy.

> **Note**
> Store in an airtight container in the fridge for up to 1 week. You can use cashews as a substitute for hemp seeds.

creamy dreamy peanut dressing

YIELD: MAKES ABOUT 1¼ CUPS

Everyone needs to have a creamy Asian-style dressing recipe in their back pocket. This one's a little spicy, a little sweet, and can be paired with anything from an Asian-style salad to a dipping sauce for spring rolls. Make sure to use a fresh jar of runny, natural peanut butter—it will make the sauce easier to stir! Skip the peanut butters with sugar and oils, and instead, look for a jar that contains only peanuts in the ingredients. Use tahini or sunflower butter for a nut-free version.

Use for **Adzuki Bean Salad, Spring Roll Salad**

prep time:
5 minutes

½ cup natural peanut butter

3 tbsp coconut aminos

1 tbsp soy sauce

2 tbsp rice vinegar

2 tbsp sriracha

½ tsp garlic powder

¼ tsp ginger powder

1 tbsp toasted sesame oil

¼ tsp salt

1. To a bowl, add all the ingredients and ⅓ cup water. Whisk together until well combined. Enjoy!

Note

Store extra dressing in an airtight container in the fridge for up to 2 weeks.

peanut butter

garlic
powder

ginger
powder

salt

coconut
aminos

sesame oil

rice vinegar

soy sauce

sriracha

maple syrup

extra-virgin olive oil

poppy seeds

Dijon mustard

white wine vinegar

salt

shallot

yogurt

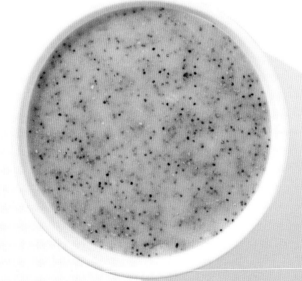

perfect poppy seed dressing

YIELD: MAKES ABOUT 1 ½ CUPS

My husband tried this dressing and said it was his favorite dressing that I've ever made. It's creamy, light, and perfect for a salad or as a dip for veggies. This Perfect Poppy Seed Dressing is made with vegan yogurt, which is the secret to a creamy, dairy-free dressing.

Use for **Malibu Salad, Superfood Brain-Booster Salad**

prep time:
5 minutes

¼ cup white wine vinegar

½ cup extra-virgin olive oil

2 tbsp plain vegan yogurt

2 tbsp maple syrup

2 tsp minced shallot

1 tsp Dijon mustard

¼ tsp salt

1 ½ tbsp poppy seeds

1. To a small bowl, add the vinegar, olive oil, yogurt, maple syrup, shallot, mustard, and salt. Whisk or emulsify with a handheld frother or immersion blender until smooth.

2. Add the poppy seeds to the dressing and stir to combine. Enjoy!

> **Note**
> Store in the fridge for up to 1 week
> in an airtight container.

italiangirl dressing

YIELD: MAKES ABOUT 1 CUP

I used to beg my parents to go out to Italian restaurants for dinner because, of course, I loved the pasta, but also because I loved the house Italian salad dressing. Make this, and you'll have your own Italian restaurant dressing that you can bottle up right at home. Use it to marinate your proteins, dress your greens, or even dip crusty bread.

Use for **The Italian, Pizza Night Salad**

prep time:
5 minutes

⅓ cup extra-virgin olive oil

2 tbsp white wine vinegar

1 tbsp lemon juice

1 tsp Dijon mustard

1 tsp maple syrup

1 tsp dried oregano

¼ tsp salt

¼ tsp garlic powder or 1 tsp minced fresh garlic

2 tbsp finely chopped fresh Italian parsley

Freshly ground black pepper, to taste

1. In a small bowl or jar, add all the ingredients. Whisk or shake well to combine, and enjoy!

Note

Store in the fridge for up to 2 weeks in an airtight container or a jar.

lemon juice

maple syrup

black pepper

extra-virgin olive oil

white wine vinegar

Dijon mustard

salt

garlic

dried oregano

parsley

salsa

cumin

salt

paprika

cashews

lime

cilantro

fiesta dressing

YIELD: MAKES ABOUT 2 CUPS

If salsa and sour cream got married, this Fiesta Dressing would be their baby!
It also makes a great dip for tortilla chips or as a healthy nacho topping.

Use for **The Fiesta Chop**

prep time:
10 minutes

1 cup tomato-based salsa
(your favorite kind!)

1½ cups cashews

Juice of 1 lime

¼ cup fresh cilantro

½ tsp ground cumin

½ tsp smoked paprika

1 tsp salt

1. To a blender, add all the ingredients and ⅓ cup water. Blend until smooth.

> **Note**
> Store in the fridge for up to a week in an airtight container for optimal freshness! If you do not have a high-speed blender like a Vitamix, boil cashews for 5 minutes to soften them before blending.

cha cha chimichurri

YIELD: MAKES ABOUT 1 CUP

I like to think of chimichurri as a parsley pesto. It's bright, fresh, zesty, easy to make, and delicious on anything from salads to tofu steaks. This is a good recipe to have in your back pocket.

Use for **Roasted Carrot Salad**

prep time:
10 minutes

½ cup extra-virgin olive oil

¼ cup red wine vinegar

1 cup fresh parsley

4 cloves garlic

1 tsp salt

½ tsp ground black pepper

Optional add-ins:

Red chili flakes (make it spicy!)

Dried oregano

Shallot

1. To a food processor, add all the ingredients and pulse until blended but not too smooth—you want to be able to see pieces of parsley still.

Note

Store in an airtight container in the fridge for up to 4 days. The food processor makes this easy to combine, but you can chop the parsley and garlic and then whisk the ingredients together by hand if you like.

red wine vinegar

red chili flakes

dried oregano

extra-virgin olive oil

black pepper

garlic

salt

parsley

shallot

maple syrup

balsamic vinegar

black pepper

Dijon mustard

salt

extra-virgin olive oil

balsamic baby

YIELD: MAKES ABOUT ½ CUP

This easy balsamic is a good one to keep handy. This is probably my
most-used salad dressing due to its simplicity and versatility.
Use it for everything from pasta salads to quinoa salads.

Use for **Are You Figgin' Kidding Me?, Delicata Squash Salad,
The Fall Edit, Wild Rice Salad**

prep time:
5 minutes

¼ cup extra-virgin olive oil

3 tbsp balsamic vinegar

1 tbsp maple syrup

1 tsp Dijon mustard

½ tsp salt

¼ tsp ground black pepper

1. Add all the ingredients to a jar or a bowl, and
shake or whisk until fully combined. Enjoy!

> **Note**
> Store in the fridge for up to 2 weeks
> in an airtight container or a jar.

avocado cilantro lime dressing

YIELD: MAKES ABOUT 2½ CUPS

This dressing is a game changer—it's almost drinkable! It's creamy, zesty, spicy, and it takes only 3 minutes to make. If you have a nut allergy, substitute hemp seeds for the cashews. Not only is this dressing beyond yummy, but it's also packed with healthy fats, which are great for glowing skin, strong nails, and thick hair. Use as a dressing in taco salads and bowls, as a sauce for burritos, and even as a dip for chips.

Use for **Cuban Cutie, Layered Mexican Salad**

prep time:
10 minutes

2 ripe avocados, pits and skins removed

¼ cup cashews or hemp seeds

¼ cup lime juice

¼ cup avocado oil or extra-virgin olive oil

2 tbsp apple cider vinegar

1 cup fresh cilantro

3 cloves garlic

2 tbsp marinated jalapeño slices

1 tbsp jalapeño brine

2 tsp salt

1. To a blender, add all the ingredients and ¼ cup water. Blend on high until creamy.

> **Note**
> Store in an airtight container in the fridge for up to 2 days. Add plastic wrap to the top of the sauce inside the container to keep it from browning.

avocado oil

jalapeños + brine

apple
cider
vinegar

cilantro

garlic

cashews

salt

avocados

lime

maple syrup

salt

ginger

garlic

carrots

rice vinegar

sesame oil

extra-virgin olive oil

carrot ginger dressing

YIELD: MAKES ABOUT 1⅓ CUPS

When I go out for sushi, my favorite condiment to order is a carrot ginger dressing. I dip my sushi in it, get it on my salads, and ask for a to-go order of it—I am a carrot ginger–dressing monster. I decided I needed to make my own version so I could enjoy it at home. It's fresh, easy, sweet, and a little spicy, and it's perfect on everything from Asian-inspired noodle salads to sushi bowls.

Use for **California Roll in a Bowl**

prep time:
10 minutes

⅓ cup extra-virgin olive oil

3 tbsp rice vinegar

2 large carrots, peeled and cut into chunks

1 thumb of fresh ginger (1-inch piece)

2 garlic cloves

1 tsp toasted sesame oil

1 tsp salt

1 tsp maple syrup

1. To a blender or food processor, add all the ingredients and blend until combined. Feel free to blend until it's smooth or leave it with more of a textured consistency. Both ways are delish!

> **Note**
> Store the dressing in an airtight container in the fridge for up to 2 weeks.

walnutty pesto dressing

YIELD: MAKES ABOUT ¾ CUP

Walnuts are one of the healthiest nuts you can eat. Filled with omega-3 fatty acids, fiber, magnesium, and folate, they are nutrient powerhouses. Adding walnuts to a pesto sauce is a great way to get in those healthy, brain-loving fats. Make this in your blender, with a mortar and pestle, or in a food processor. I personally like to use a food processor—it's easy and keeps a classic pesto texture.

Use for **Plant-Goddess Tortellini, Tuscan Butter-Bean Salad**

prep time:
10 minutes

2 cups fresh basil, tightly packed

½ cup extra-virgin olive oil

½ cup walnuts (optional to toast them)

1 tbsp nutritional yeast

2 tbsp lemon juice

2 cloves garlic

½ tsp salt

1. To a food processor, add all the ingredients and blend until combined.

Note

Store in an airtight container in the fridge for up to 4 days.

lemon juice

salt

extra-virgin olive oil

nutritional yeast

garlic

basil

walnuts

mayonnaise

lime juice

black pepper

avocado oil

cayenne

salt

yogurt

cumin

nutritional yeast

paprika

chili powder

garlic powder

pickled jalapeño

elote dressing

YIELD: MAKES ABOUT 2 CUPS

Creamy, dreamy, and a dressing you'd never know is dairy-free. This Elote Dressing is super easy to make and is so incredibly yummy. I even like to use it as a taco topping!

Use for **Summer Elote Pasta Salad**

prep time:
10 minutes

- ¾ cup plain vegan yogurt
- 3 tbsp vegan mayonnaise
- 2 tbsp lime juice
- 1 tbsp avocado oil
- 2 tbsp water
- 2 tbsp nutritional yeast
- 1 tsp ground cumin
- ½ tsp smoked paprika
- ¼ tsp garlic powder
- 2 tbsp minced pickled jalapeño
- 1 tsp chili powder
- 1 tsp salt
- Pinch of ground black pepper
- Pinch of cayenne

1. To a medium bowl or blender, add all the ingredients, then whisk or blend until combined.

> **Note**
> Store in an airtight container in the fridge for up to 4 days.

valleygirl ranch dressing

YIELD: MAKES ABOUT 2 CUPS

Ranch: either you love it or you hate it. I, for one, am obsessed with it!
I grew up putting it on everything, from my pizza to my fries.

Use for **BBQ Tofu Chopped Salad, Buffalo "Chicken" Salad, Wedgie Veggie Salad**

prep time:
5 minutes

1 cup cashews

¾ cup unsweetened plant milk

2 tbsp extra-virgin olive oil

2 tbsp lemon juice

1 tsp garlic powder

1 tsp dried parsley

2 tsp dried dill

1 tsp dried chives

¼ tsp onion powder

1 tsp salt

Freshly ground black pepper,
to taste

1. To a blender, add all the ingredients and blend until completely smooth.

> **Note**
> Store in an airtight container in
> the fridge for up to 2 weeks.

extra-virgin
olive oil

black pepper

garlic powder

dried parsley

dried chives

dried dill

salt

unsweetened
plant milk

cashews

lemon juice

onion powder

chipotle peppers

lime juice

cashews

maple syrup

salt

garlic

black pepper

nondairy milk

chipotle ranch

YIELD: MAKES ABOUT 2 CUPS

Either you're a ranch girl or you're not. I'm a ranch girl. Give me *all* the creamy dressings. If you like a little spice and you're a ranch lover, you're in for a treat with this recipe. Use this delicious dressing for pasta salad, as a dip for a panini or a wrap, or as a great dip for pita chips or veggies! It's versatile and easy to make.

Use for **Chipotle Chica Salad, Chopped Kale + Crispy Tofu Wrap, Wedgie Veggie Salad**

prep time:
10 minutes

1 cup cashews

3 chipotle peppers
in adobo sauce

3 cloves garlic

1 tsp maple syrup

2 tbsp lime juice

½ cup nondairy milk

1 tsp salt

½ tsp ground black pepper

1. To a high-speed blender, like a Vitamix, add all the ingredients and ½ cup water. Blend on high until completely smooth.

> **Note**
> Store in an airtight container in the fridge for up to 1 week. If you don't have a high-speed blender, boil the cashews for 5 to 10 minutes before blending in a standard blender on high.

honeyless mustard

YIELD: MAKES ABOUT ½ CUP

Honey mustard dressing is one of those classic dressings. For those of you who don't like honey, here's a perfect alternative. Enjoy this drizzled over bowls, with tofu chicken tenders, as a dip for chips, or on a salad.

Use for **Chopped Kale + Crispy Tofu Wrap**

prep time:
5 minutes

¼ cup maple syrup

¼ cup Dijon mustard

1 tbsp white vinegar

¼ tsp garlic powder

Generous pinch of salt

1. In a medium bowl, add all the ingredients and mix together.

> **Note**
> Store in the fridge for up to 2 weeks in an airtight container.

maple syrup

garlic powder

white vinegar

salt

Dijon mustard

black pepper

salt

cumin

lemon juice

Dijon mustard

turmeric

extra-virgin olive oil

tahini

golden goddess sunshine dressing

YIELD: MAKES ABOUT ⅔ CUP

This dressing is not only delicious but also has inflammation-reducing properties from the turmeric. It's creamy, goes well on almost any kind of salad or bowl, and is a great way to get those healthy fats in from the dreamy tahini.

Use for **Golden Goddess Salad**

prep time:
5 minutes

⅓ cup extra-virgin olive oil

¼ cup tahini

1 tsp Dijon mustard

2 tbsp lemon juice

1 tsp ground cumin

½ tsp ground turmeric

1 tsp salt

¼ tsp ground black pepper

1. In a bowl, whisk all the ingredients together. Enjoy!

Note

Keep in the fridge for up to 1 week in an airtight container.

---

green goodness dressing

YIELD: MAKES ABOUT 1¾ CUPS

My version of a green goddess dressing is made without mayonnaise and dairy.
It is packed with herbs, greens, and avocado to make a creamy, vibrant dressing
that can be paired with almost any salad or bowl. You can even use it as a
dip or as a sauce for pasta!

Use for **Green Vibes–Only Salad, Rooting for You**

prep time:
5 minutes

1 ripe avocado, pit and skin removed

¼ cup plain vegan yogurt or vegan mayonnaise

⅓ cup extra-virgin olive oil or avocado oil

¼ cup lemon juice

1 clove garlic

2 tbsp walnuts

¼ cup fresh parsley

½ cup fresh basil

¼ cup fresh cilantro

2 tbsp fresh chives

1 tsp Dijon mustard

1 tsp salt

Pinch of ground black pepper

1. To a blender, add all the ingredients, then blend on high. If needed, add 1 to 2 tablespoons of water to thin the dressing.

Note
Store in the fridge for up to 3 days in an airtight container.

lemon juice

avocado

cilantro

black pepper

extra-virgin
olive oil

yogurt

parsley

salt

garlic

Dijon mustard

walnuts

basil

chives

tahini

maple syrup

garlic powder

black pepper

salt

balsamic vinegar

extra-virgin
olive oil

balsamic tahini dressing

YIELD: MAKES ABOUT ¾ CUP

This dressing blends a traditional balsamic vinaigrette with a creamy tahini element.
Tahini is a great hack to make a dressing creamy without using mayo or dairy!
Tahini is made from sesame seeds and is packed with healthy fats!

Use for **Gut-Loving Farro Salad, Health-Nut Salad, Superfood Brain-Booster Salad, Wild Rice Salad, The Zen Bowl**

prep time:
5 minutes

4 tbsp runny tahini

3 tbsp extra-virgin olive oil

½ tsp garlic powder

1 tsp maple syrup

3 tbsp balsamic vinegar

Salt and ground black pepper, to taste

1. To a bowl or a jar, add all the ingredients and 2 tablespoons of water. Whisk or shake until well combined.

Note

Store in an airtight container or a jar in the fridge for up to 2 weeks. Add 1 to 2 more tablespoons of water if it's too thick.

Acknowledgments

There's a whole lot that goes into writing a book and it's safe to say I couldn't have done it without my village.

Taylor, my right-hand woman here at HealthyGirl Kitchen, I am forever grateful to you. Your creativity, positivity, upbeat can-do attitude, dedication, recipe development contributions, and willingness to always eat and sample food with me has not gone unnoticed. Love ya more than salad. Brandon, thank you for being my co-food stylist on the book cover. Your artistic eye and design skills are unmatched.

Alex Rigby, you are an incredibly gifted editor. Thank you for believing in me (again). You shared in my vision for this second book and you along with the rest of the DK team helped me to execute my dream of a salad book perfectly.

Ari, my handsome, very special, hardworking husband, and best dad ever to our little Aidan, thank you times a thousand for taking on the very important job of being lead photographer of the book for the second time. I know you missed a lot of days at your office, but know I appreciate you more than words can express. Thank you for taste-testing all my dressings and recipes even though you don't like the ones with yogurt or mushrooms.

A huge thank-you goes out to my amazing team at Digital Renegades, who all work around the clock representing myself and the HealthyGirl brand, and help me accomplish my dreams.

To my gorgeous lifelong girlfriend Cammy, who flew all the way to Florida from Michigan to do my makeup for the cookbook lifestyle photoshoot, you are the best. Thank you for making me feel so confident and beautiful.

Last but certainly not least, thank you to my HealthyGirl community. Your continuous support makes me eternally grateful. Because of your support of my first cookbook, I was able to create a second one. I owe it all to you!

Index

About the Author

I am a self-proclaimed salad lover. From the time I was eight years old, my order at our local metro-Detroit Greek diner was a Greek salad with extra feta, extra pickled beets, crispy onions, and grilled pita on the side. I'd ask the waiter to please make it "double chopped" with an extra side of dressing. I'd also get a side of lemon rice soup, and well, that was my definition of the perfect meal. When I think back, that chopped Greek salad was indeed a "life-changing salad."

Every night, my mom made sure we had family dinner. No matter what we were eating, she always included a simple salad. Her classic combination was romaine, cherry tomatoes, cucumbers, bell peppers, and carrots. I liked the predictability of my mom's nightly salads. My favorite part was choosing a dressing. I'd argue a good dressing is the most important part of a salad. She offered a variety of bottled dressings from which we could choose, from French dressing and balsamic vinaigrette to ranch. If there were ever leftovers in the large salad bowl at the end of our meal, I'd ask to finish them, and my mom would let me eat out of the bowl.

When I transitioned to a plant-based diet my freshman year of college, I found it almost impossible to order a decent salad that was filling and hearty from a restaurant. Sure, I could find a salad with iceberg and tomatoes, but I wanted more. Out of desperation for satiating plant-based meals, I slowly grew into a more creative cook in my college apartment.

My love for healthy cooking (and eating) grew by the day. After starting my life-changing salad series on social media in 2021—and hundreds of millions of views later—I am so proud (and literally so freaking excited) to have written this book for you. This will be your go-to book for all things salad.

A lot has changed since my first book. I AM A MAMA! I have a beautiful son, Aidan. He completes my heart. His favorite foods are noodles, raisins, and sweet potato fries. He's got the best smile, dimples, and is the silliest, sweetest little guy ever. My husband, Ari, and I renovated our dream home and now live in Delray Beach, Florida, as a little family.

As a mom, cooking and preparing meals looks a little different these days. I need quick, easy, realistic, and leftover friendly. These recipes are perfect for busy people, on-the-go girlies, moms, and health-conscious individuals who want to include more plants and eat more salads.